THE PELICAN SHAKESPEARE
GENERAL EDITORS

STEPHEN ORGEL
A. R. BRAUNMULLER

Much Ado About Nothing

Ellen Terry as Beatrice, 1891

William Shakespeare

Much Ado About Nothing

EDITED BY PETER HOLLAND

PENGUIN BOOKS

PENGUIN BOOKS

Published by the Penguin Group
Penguin Putnam Inc., 375 Hudson Street,
New York, New York 10014, U.S.A.
Penguin Books Ltd, 80 Strand, London WC2R 0RL, England
Penguin Books Australia Ltd, 250 Camberwell Road,
Camberwell, Victoria 3124, Australia
Penguin Books Canada Ltd, 10 Alcorn Avenue,
Toronto, Ontario, Canada M4V 3B2
Penguin Books India (P) Ltd, 11 Community Centre,
Panchsheel Park, New Delhi—110 017, India
Penguin Books (N.Z.) Ltd, Cnr Rosedale and Airborne Roads,
Albany, Auckland, New Zealand
Penguin Books (South Africa) (Pty) Ltd, 24 Sturdee Avenue,
Rosebank, Johannesburg 2196, South Africa

Penguin Books Ltd, Registered Offices:
Harmondsworth, Middlesex, England

Much Ado About Nothing edited by Josephine Waters Bennett
published in the United States of America
in Penguin Books 1958
Revised edition published 1971
This new edition edited by Peter Holland published 1999

7   9   10   8

Copyright © Penguin Books Inc., 1958, 1971
Copyright © Penguin Putnam Inc., 1999
All rights reserved

ISBN 0-14-07.1480-4

Printed in the United States of America
Set in Garamond
Designed by Virginia Norey

Contents

Publisher's Note

IT IS ALMOST half a century since the first volumes of the Pelican Shakespeare appeared under the general editorship of Alfred Harbage. The fact that a new edition, rather than simply a revision, has been undertaken reflects the profound changes textual and critical studies of Shakespeare have undergone in the past twenty years. For the new Pelican series, the texts of the plays and poems have been thoroughly revised in accordance with recent scholarship, and in some cases have been entirely reedited. New introductions and notes have been provided in all the volumes. But the new Shakespeare is also designed as a successor to the original series; the previous editions have been taken into account, and the advice of the previous editors has been solicited where it was feasible to do so.

Certain textual features of the new Pelican Shakespeare should be particularly noted. All lines are numbered that contain a word, phrase, or allusion explained in the glossarial notes. In addition, for convenience, every tenth line is also numbered, in italics when no annotation is indicated. The intrusive and often inaccurate place headings inserted by early editors are omitted (as is becoming standard practice), but for the convenience of those who miss them, an indication of locale now appears as the first item in the annotation of each scene.

In the interest of both elegance and utility, each speech prefix is set in a separate line when the speaker's lines are in verse, except when those words form the second half of a verse line. Thus the verse form of the speech is kept visually intact. What is printed as verse and what is printed as prose has, in general, the authority of the original texts. Departures from the original texts in this regard have only the authority of editorial tradition and the judgment of the Pelican editors; and, in a few instances, are admittedly arbitrary.

The Theatrical World

ECONOMIC REALITIES determined the theatrical world in which Shakespeare's plays were written, performed, and received. For centuries in England, the primary theatrical tradition was nonprofessional. Craft guilds (or "mysteries") provided religious drama – mystery plays – as part of the celebration of religious and civic festivals, and schools and universities staged classical and neoclassical drama in both Latin and English as part of their curricula. In these forms, drama was established and socially acceptable. Professional theater, in contrast, existed on the margins of society. The acting companies were itinerant; playhouses could be any available space – the great halls of the aristocracy, town squares, civic halls, inn yards, fair booths, or open fields – and income was sporadic, dependent on the passing of the hat or on the bounty of local patrons. The actors, moreover, were considered little better than vagabonds, constantly in danger of arrest or expulsion.

In the late 1560s and 1570s, however, English professional theater began to gain respectability. Wealthy aristocrats fond of drama – the Lord Admiral, for example, or the Lord Chamberlain – took acting companies under their protection so that the players technically became members of their households and were no longer subject to arrest as homeless or masterless men. Permanent theaters were first built at this time as well, allowing the companies to control and charge for entry to their performances.

Shakespeare's livelihood, and the stunning artistic explosion in which he participated, depended on pragmatic and architectural effort. Professional theater requires ways to restrict access to its offerings; if it does not, and admission fees cannot be charged, the actors do not get paid, the costumes go to a pawnbroker, and there is no such thing as a professional, ongoing theatrical tradition. The answer to that economic need arrived in the late 1560s and 1570s with the creation of the so-called public or amphitheater playhouse. Recent discoveries indicate that the precursor of the Globe playhouse in London (where Shakespeare's mature plays were presented) and the Rose theater (which presented Christopher Marlowe's plays and some of Shakespeare's earliest ones) was the Red Lion theater of 1567. Archaeological studies of the foundations of the Rose and Globe theaters have revealed that the open-air theater of the 1590s and later was probably a polygonal building with fourteen to twenty or twenty-four sides, multistoried, from 75 to 100 feet in diameter, with a raised, partly covered "thrust" stage that projected into a group of standing patrons, or "groundlings," and a covered gallery, seating up to 2,500 or more (very crowded) spectators.

These theaters might have been about half full on any given day, though the audiences were larger on holidays or when a play was advertised, as old and new were, through printed playbills posted around London. The metropolitan area's late-Tudor, early-Stuart population (circa 1590-1620) has been estimated at about 150,000 to 250,000. It has been supposed that in the mid-1590s there were about 15,000 spectators per week at the public theaters; thus, as many as 10 percent of the local population went to the theater regularly. Consequently, the theaters' repertories – the plays available for this experienced and frequent audience – had to change often: in the month between September 15 and October 15, 1595, for instance, the Lord Admiral's Men performed twenty-eight times in eighteen different plays.

Since natural light illuminated the amphitheaters' stages, performances began between noon and two o'clock and ran without a break for two or three hours. They often concluded with a jig, a fencing display, or some other nondramatic exhibition. Weather conditions deter-

mined the season for the amphitheaters: plays were performed every day (including Sundays, sometimes, to cler-
ical dismay) except during Lent – the forty days before
Easter – or periods of plague, or sometimes during the
summer months when law courts were not in session and
the most affluent members of the audience were not in
London.

To a modern theatergoer, an amphitheater stage like
that of the Rose or Globe would appear an unfamiliar mix-
ture of plainness and elaborate decoration. Much of the
structure was carved or painted, sometimes to imitate
marble; elsewhere, as under the canopy projecting over the
stage, to represent the stars and the zodiac. Appropriate
painted canvas pictures (of Jerusalem, for example, if the
play was set in that city) were apparently hung on the wall
behind the acting area, and tragedies were accompanied by
black hangings, presumably something like crepe festoons
or bunting. Although these theaters did not employ what
we would call scenery, early modern spectators saw numerous large props, such as the "bar" at which a prisoner stood
during a trial, the "mossy bank" where lovers reclined,
an arbor for amorous conversation, a chariot, gallows,
tables, trees, beds, thrones, writing desks, and so forth.
Audiences might learn a scene's location from a sign (reading "Athens," for example) carried across the stage (as in
Bertolt Brecht's twentieth-century productions). Equally
captivating (and equally irritating to the theater's enemies)
were the rich costumes and personal props the actors used:
the most valuable items in the surviving theatrical invento-
ries are the swords, gowns, robes, crowns, and other items
worn or carried by the performers.

Magic appealed to Shakespeare's audiences as much as
it does to us today, and the theater exploited many decep-
tive and spectacular devices. A winch in the loft above the
stage, called "the heavens," could lower and raise actors
playing gods, goddesses, and other supernatural figures to
and from the main acting area, just as one or more trap-
doors permitted entrances and exits to and from the area,

called "hell," beneath the stage. Actors wore elementary makeup such as wigs, false beards, and face paint, and they employed pig's bladders filled with animal blood to make wounds seem more real. They had rudimentary but effective ways of pretending to behead or hang a person. Supernumeraries (stagehands or actors not needed in a particular scene) could make thunder sounds (by shaking a metal sheet or rolling an iron ball down a chute) and show lightning (by blowing inflammable resin through tubes into a flame). Elaborate fireworks enhanced the effects of dragons flying through the air or imitated such celestial phenomena as comets, shooting stars, and multiple suns. Horses' hoofbeats, bells (located perhaps in the tower above the stage), trumpets and drums, clocks, cannon shots and gunshots, and the like were common sound effects. And the music of viols, cornets, oboes, and recorders was a regular feature of theatrical performances.

For two relatively brief spans, from the late 1570s to 1590 and from 1599 to 1614, the amphitheaters competed with the so-called private, or indoor, theaters, which originated as, or later represented themselves as, educational institutions training boys as singers for church services and court performances. These indoor theaters had two features that were distinct from the amphitheaters': their personnel and their playing spaces. The amphitheaters' adult companies included both adult men, who played the male roles, and boys, who played the female roles; the private, or indoor, theater companies, on the other hand, were entirely composed of boys aged about 8 to 16, who were, or could pretend to be, candidates for singers in a church or a royal boys' choir. (Until 1660, professional theatrical companies included no women.) The playing space would appear much more familiar to modern audiences than the long-vanished amphitheaters; the later indoor theaters were, in fact, the ancestors of the typical modern theater. They were enclosed spaces, usually rectangular, with the stage filling one end of the rectangle and the audience arrayed in seats or benches across (and sometimes lining) the building's longer axis. These spaces staged plays less frequently than the public theaters (perhaps only once a week) and held far fewer spectators than the amphitheaters: about 200 to 600, as opposed to 2,500 or more. Fewer patrons mean a smaller gross income, unless each pays more. Not surprisingly, then, private theaters charged higher prices than the amphitheaters, probably sixpence, as opposed to a penny for the cheapest entry.

Protected from the weather, the indoor theaters presented plays later in the day than the amphitheaters, and used artificial illumination – candles in sconces or candelabra. But candles melt, and need replacing, snuffing, and trimming, and these practical requirements may have been part of the reason the indoor theaters introduced breaks in the performance, the intermission so dear to the heart of theatergoers and to the pocketbooks of theater concessionaires ever since. Whether motivated by the need to tend to the candles or by the entrepreneurs' wishing to sell oranges and liquor, or both, the indoor theaters eventually established the modern convention of the non-continuous performance. In the early modern "private" theater, musical performances apparently filled the intermissions, which in Stuart theater jargon seem to have been called "acts."

At the end of the first decade of the seventeenth century, the distinction between public amphitheaters and private indoor companies ceased. For various cultural, political, and economic reasons, individual companies gained control of both the public, open-air theaters and the indoor ones, and companies mixing adult men and boys took over the formerly "private" theaters. Despite the death of the boys' companies and of their highly innovative theaters (for which such luminous playwrights as Ben Jonson, George Chapman, and John Marston wrote), their playing spaces and conventions had an immense impact on subsequent plays: not merely for the intervals (which stressed the artistic and architectonic importance of "acts"), but also because they introduced political and social satire as a popular dramatic ingredient, even in tragedy, and a wider range of actorly effects, encouraged by their more intimate playing spaces.

Even the briefest sketch of the Shakespearean theatrical world would be incomplete without some comment on the social and cultural dimensions of theaters and playing in the period. In an intensely hierarchical and status-conscious society, professional actors and their ventures had hardly any respectability; as we have indicated, to protect themselves against laws designed to curb vagabondage and the increase of masterless men, actors resorted to the near-fiction that they were the servants of noble masters, and wore their distinctive livery. Hence the company for which Shakespeare wrote in the 1590s called itself the Lord Chamberlain's Men and pretended that the public, money-getting performances were in fact rehearsals for private per-formances before that high court official. From 1598, the Privy Council had licensed theatrical companies, and after 1603, with the accession of King James I, the companies gained explicit royal protection, just as the Queen's Men had for a time under Queen Elizabeth. The Chamberlain's Men became the King's Men, and the other companies were patronized by the other members of the royal family.

These designations were legal fictions that half-concealed an important economic and social develop-ment, the evolution away from the theater's organization on the model of the guild, a self-regulating confraternity of individual artisans, into a proto-capitalist organization. Shakespeare's company became a joint-stock company, where persons who supplied capital and, in some cases, such as Shakespeare's, capital and talent, employed them-selves and others in earning a return on that capital. This development meant that actors and theater companies were outside both the traditional guild structures, which required some form of civic or royal charter, and the feu-dal household organization of master-and-servant. This anomalous, maverick social and economic condition made theater companies practically unruly and potentially even dangerous; consequently, numerous official bodies – including the London metropolitan and ecclesiastical authorities as well as, occasionally, the royal court itself – tried, without much success, to control and even to disband them.

Public officials had good reason to want to close the theaters: they were attractive nuisances – they drew often riotous crowds, they were always noisy, and they could be politically offensive and socially insubordinate. Until the Civil War, however, anti-theatrical forces failed to shut down professional theater, for many reasons – limited surveillance and few police powers, tensions or outright hostilities among the agencies that sought to check or channel theatrical activity, and lack of clear policies for control. Another reason must have been the theaters' undeniable popularity. Curtailing any activity enjoyed by such a substantial percentage of the population was difficult, as various Roman emperors attempting to limit circuses had learned, and the Tudor-Stuart audience was not merely large, it was socially diverse and included women. The prevalence of public entertainment in this period has been underestimated. In fact, fairs, holidays, games, sporting events, the equivalent of modern parades, freak shows, and street exhibitions all abounded, but the theater was the most widely and frequently available entertainment to which people of every class had access. That fact helps account both for its quantity and for the fear and anger it aroused.

WILLIAM SHAKESPEARE OF STRATFORD-UPON-AVON, GENTLEMAN

Many people have said that we know very little about William Shakespeare's life – pinheads and postcards are often mentioned as appropriately tiny surfaces on which to record the available information. More imaginatively and perhaps more correctly, Ralph Waldo Emerson wrote, "Shakespeare is the only biographer of Shakespeare. . . . So far from Shakespeare's being the least known, he is the one person in all modern history fully known to us."

In fact, we know more about Shakespeare's life than we do about almost any other English writer's of his era. His last will and testament (dated March 25, 1616) survives, as do numerous legal contracts and court documents involving Shakespeare as principal or witness, and parish records in Stratford and London. Shakespeare appears quite often in official records of King James's royal court, and of course Shakespeare's name appears on numerous title pages and in the written and recorded words of his literary contemporaries Robert Greene, Henry Chettle, Francis Meres, John Davies of Hereford, Ben Jonson, and many others. Indeed, if we make due allowance for the bloating of modern, run-of-the-mill bureaucratic records, more information has survived over the past four hundred years about William Shakespeare of Stratford-upon-Avon, Warwickshire, than is likely to survive in the next four hundred years about any reader of these words.

What we do not have are entire categories of information – Shakespeare's private letters or diaries, drafts and revisions of poems and plays, critical prefaces or essays, commendatory verse for other writers' works, or instructions guiding his fellow actors in their performances, for instance – that we imagine would help us understand and appreciate his surviving writings. For all we know, many such data never existed as written records. Many literary and theatrical critics, not knowing what might once have existed, more or less cheerfully accept the situation; some even make a theoretical virtue of it by claiming that such data are irrelevant to understanding and interpreting the plays and poems.

So, what do we know about William Shakespeare, the man responsible for thirty-seven or perhaps more plays, more than 150 sonnets, two lengthy narrative poems, and some shorter poems?

While many families by the name of Shakespeare (or some variant spelling) can be identified in the English Midlands as far back as the twelfth century, it seems likely that the dramatist's grandfather, Richard, moved to Snitterfield, a town not far from Stratford-upon-Avon, sometime before 1529. In Snitterfield, Richard Shakespeare leased farmland from the very wealthy Robert Arden. By 1552, Richard's son John had moved to a large house on Henley Street in Stratford-upon-Avon, the house that stands today as "The Birthplace." In Stratford, John Shakespeare traded as a glover, dealt in wool, and lent money at interest; he also served in a variety of civic posts, including "High Bailiff," the municipality's equivalent of mayor. In 1557, he married Robert Arden's youngest daughter, Mary. Mary and John had four sons – William was the oldest – and four daughters, of whom only Joan outlived her most celebrated sibling. William was baptized (an event entered in the Stratford parish church records) on April 26, 1564, and it has become customary, without any good factual support, to suppose he was born on April 23, which happens to be the feast day of Saint George, patron saint of England, and is also the date on which he died, in 1616. Shakespeare married Anne Hathaway in 1582, when he was eighteen and she was twenty-six; their first child was born five months later. It has been generally assumed that the marriage was enforced and subsequently unhappy, but these are only assumptions; it has been estimated, for instance, that up to one third of Elizabethan brides were pregnant when they married. Anne and William Shakespeare had three children: Susanna, who married a prominent local physician, John Hall; and the twins Hamnet, who died young in 1596, and Judith, who married Thomas Quiney – apparently a rather shady individual. The name Hamnet was unusual but not unique: he and his twin sister were named for their godparents, Shakespeare's neighbors Hamnet and Judith Sadler. Shakespeare's father died in 1601 (the year of *Hamlet*), and Mary Arden Shakespeare died in 1608 (the year of *Coriolanus*). William Shakespeare's last surviving direct descendant was his granddaughter Elizabeth Hall, who died in 1670.

Between the birth of the twins in 1585 and a clear reference to Shakespeare as a practicing London dramatist in Robert Greene's sensationalizing, satiric pamphlet, *Greene's Groatsworth of Wit* (1592), there is no record of where William Shakespeare was or what he was doing. These seven so-called lost years have been imaginatively filled by scholars and other students of Shakespeare: some think he traveled to Italy, or fought in the Low Countries, or studied law or medicine, or worked as an apprentice actor/writer, and so on to even more fanciful possibilities. Whatever the biographical facts for those "lost" years, Greene's nasty remarks in 1592 testify to professional envy and to the fact that Shakespeare already had a successful career in London. Speaking to his fellow playwrights, Greene warns both generally and specifically:

> . . . trust them [actors] not: for there is an upstart crow, beautified with our feathers, that with his tiger's heart wrapped in a player's hide supposes he is as well able to bombast out a blank verse as the best of you; and being an absolute Johannes Factotum, is in his own conceit the only Shake-scene in a country.

The passage mimics a line from *3 Henry VI* (hence the play must have been performed before Greene wrote) and seems to say that "Shake-scene" is both actor and playwright, a jack-of-all-trades. That same year, Henry Chettle protested Greene's remarks in *Kind-Heart's Dream,* and each of the next two years saw the publication of poems – *Venus and Adonis* and *The Rape of Lucrece,* respectively – publicly ascribed to (and dedicated by) Shakespeare. Early in 1595 he was named as one of the senior members of a prominent acting company, the Lord Chamberlain's Men, when they received payment for court performances during the 1594 Christmas season.

Clearly, Shakespeare had achieved both success and reputation in London. In 1596, upon Shakespeare's application, the College of Arms granted his father the now-familiar coat of arms he had taken the first steps to obtain almost twenty years before, and in 1598, John's son – now permitted to call himself "gentleman" – took a 10 percent share in the new Globe playhouse. In 1597, he bought a substantial bourgeois house, called New Place, in Stratford – the garden remains, but Shakespeare's house, several times rebuilt, was torn down in 1759 – and over the next few years Shakespeare spent large sums buying land and making other investments in the town and its environs. Though he worked in London, his family remained in Stratford, and he seems always to have considered Stratford the home he would eventually return to. Something approaching a disinterested appreciation of Shakespeare's popular and professional status appears in Francis Meres's *Palladis Tamia* (1598), a not especially imaginative and perhaps therefore persuasive record of literary reputations. Reviewing contemporary English writers, Meres lists the titles of many of Shakespeare's plays, including one not now known, *Love's Labor's Won,* and praises his "mellifluous & hony-tongued" "sugred Sonnets," which were then circulating in manuscript (they were first collected in 1609). Meres describes Shakespeare as "one of the best" English playwrights of both comedy and tragedy. In *Remains . . . Concerning Britain* (1605), William Camden – a more authoritative source than the imitative Meres – calls Shakespeare one of the "most pregnant witts of these our times" and joins him with such writers as Chapman, Daniel, Jonson, Marston, and Spenser. During the first decades of the seventeenth century, publishers began to attribute numerous play quartos, including some non-Shakespearean ones, to Shakespeare, either by name or initials, and we may assume that they deemed Shakespeare's name and supposed authorship, true or false, commercially attractive.

For the next ten years or so, various records show

Shakespeare's dual career as playwright and man of the theater in London, and as an important local figure in Stratford. In 1608-9 his acting company – designated the "King's Men" soon after King James had succeeded Queen Elizabeth in 1603 – rented, refurbished, and opened a small interior playing space, the Blackfriars theater, in London, and Shakespeare was once again listed as a substantial sharer in the group of proprietors of the playhouse. By May 11, 1612, however, he describes himself as a Stratford resident in a London lawsuit – an indication that he had withdrawn from day-to-day professional activity and returned to the town where he had always had his main financial interests. When Shakespeare bought a substantial residential building in London, the Blackfriars Gatehouse, close to the theater of the same name, on March 10, 1613, he is recorded as William Shakespeare "of Stratford upon Avon in the county of Warwick, gentleman," and he named several London residents as the building's trustees. Still, he continued to participate in theatrical activity: when the new Earl of Rutland needed an allegorical design to bear as a shield, or *impresa,* at the celebration of King James's Accession Day, March 24, 1613, the earl's accountant recorded a payment of 44 shillings to Shakespeare for the device with its motto.

For the last few years of his life, Shakespeare evidently concentrated his activities in the town of his birth. Most of the final records concern business transactions in Stratford, ending with the notation of his death on April 23, 1616, and burial in Holy Trinity Church, Stratford-upon-Avon.

THE QUESTION OF AUTHORSHIP

The history of ascribing Shakespeare's plays (the poems do not come up so often) to someone else began, as it continues, peculiarly. The earliest published claim that someone else wrote Shakespeare's plays appeared in an 1856 article by Delia Bacon in the American journal *Putnam's Monthly* – although an Englishman, Thomas Wilmot, had shared his doubts in private (even secretive) conversations with friends near the end of the eighteenth century. Bacon's was a sad personal history that ended in madness and poverty, but the year after her article, she published, with great difficulty and the bemused assistance of Nathaniel Hawthorne (then United States Consul in Liverpool, England), her *Philosophy of the Plays of Shakspere Unfolded*. This huge, ornately written, confusing farrago is almost unreadable; sometimes its intents, to say nothing of its arguments, disappear entirely beneath near-raving, ecstatic writing. Tumbled in with much supposed "philosophy" appear the claims that Francis Bacon (from whom Delia Bacon eventually claimed descent), Walter Ralegh, and several other contemporaries of Shakespeare's had written the plays. The book had little impact except as a ridiculed curiosity.

Once proposed, however, the issue gained momentum among people whose conviction was the greater in proportion to their ignorance of sixteenth- and seventeenth-century English literature, history, and society. Another American amateur, Catherine P. Ashmead Windle, made the next influential contribution to the cause when she published *Report to the British Museum* (1882), wherein she promised to open "the Cipher of Francis Bacon," though what she mostly offers, in the words of S. Schoenbaum, is "demented allegorizing." An entire new cottage industry grew from Windle's suggestion that the texts contain hidden, cryptographically discoverable ciphers – "clues" – to their authorship; and today there are not only books devoted to the putative ciphers, but also pamphlets, journals, and newsletters.

Although Baconians have led the pack of those seeking a substitute Shakespeare, in *"Shakespeare" Identified* (1920), J. Thomas Looney became the first published xxii ~ THE THEATRICAL WORLD

"Oxfordian" when he proposed Edward de Vere, seventeenth earl of Oxford, as the secret author of Shakespeare's plays. Also for Oxford and his "authorship" there are today dedicated societies, articles, journals, and books. Less popular candidates – Queen Elizabeth and Christopher Marlowe among them – have had adherents, but the movement seems to have divided into two main contending factions, Baconian and Oxfordian. (For further details on all the candidates for "Shakespeare," see S. Schoenbaum, *Shakespeare's Lives,* 2nd ed., 1991.)

The Baconians, the Oxfordians, and supporters of other candidates have one trait in common – they are snobs. Every pro-Bacon or pro-Oxford tract sooner or later claims that the historical William Shakespeare of Stratford-upon-Avon could not have written the plays because he could not have had the training, the university education, the experience, and indeed the imagination or background their author supposedly possessed. Only a learned genius like Bacon or an aristocrat like Oxford could have written such fine plays. (As it happens, lucky male children of the middle class had access to better education than most aristocrats in Elizabethan England – and Oxford was not particularly well educated.) Shakespeare received in the Stratford grammar school a formal education that would daunt many college graduates today; and popular rival playwrights such as the very learned Ben Jonson and George Chapman, both of whom also lacked university training, achieved great artistic success, without being taken as Bacon or Oxford.

Besides snobbery, one other quality characterizes the authorship controversy: lack of evidence. A great deal of testimony from Shakespeare's time shows that Shakespeare wrote Shakespeare's plays and that his contemporaries recognized them as distinctive and distinctly superior. (Some of that contemporary evidence is collected in E. K. Chambers, *William Shakespeare: A Study of Facts and Problems,* 2 vols., 1930.) Since that testimony comes from Shakespeare's enemies and theatrical competitors as well as from his co-workers and from the Elizabethan equivalent of literary journalists, it seems unlikely that, if any of these sources had known he was a fraud, they would have failed to record that fact.

Books About Shakespeare's Theater

Useful scholarly studies of theatrical life in Shakespeare's day include: G. E. Bentley, *The Jacobean and Caroline Stage,* 7 vols. (1941-68), and the same author's *The Professions of Dramatist and Player in Shakespeare's Time, 1590-1642* (1986); E. K. Chambers, *The Elizabethan Stage,* 4 vols. (1923); R. A. Foakes, *Illustrations of the English Stage, 1580-1642* (1985); Andrew Gurr, *The Shakespearean Stage,* 3rd ed. (1992), and the same author's *Play-going in Shakespeare's London,* 2nd ed. (1996); Edwin Nungezer, *A Dictionary of Actors* (1929); Carol Chillington Rutter, ed., *Documents of the Rose Playhouse* (1984).

Books About Shakespeare's Life

The following books provide scholarly, documented accounts of Shakespeare's life: G. E. Bentley, *Shakespeare: A Biographical Handbook* (1961); E. K. Chambers, *William Shakespeare: A Study of Facts and Problems,* 2 vols. (1930); S. Schoenbaum, *William Shakespeare: A Compact Documentary Life* (1977); and *Shakespeare's Lives,* 2nd ed. (1991), by the same author. Many scholarly editions of Shakespeare's complete works print brief compilations of essential dates and events. References to Shakespeare's works up to 1700 are collected in C. M. Ingleby et al., *The Shakespeare Allusion-Book,* rev. ed., 2 vols. (1932).

The Texts of Shakespeare

As far as we know, only one manuscript conceivably in Shakespeare's own hand may (and even this is much disputed) exist: a few pages of a play called *Sir Thomas More,* which apparently was never performed. What we do have, as later readers, performers, scholars, students, are printed texts. The earliest of these survive in two forms: quartos and folios. Quartos (from the Latin for "four") are small books, printed on sheets of paper that were then folded in fours, to make eight double-sided pages. When these were bound together, the result was a squarish, eminently portable volume that sold for the relatively small sum of sixpence (translating in modern terms to about $5.00). In folios, on the other hand, the sheets are folded only once, in half, producing large, impressive volumes taller than they are wide. This was the format for important works of philosophy, science, theology, and literature (the major precedent for a folio Shakespeare was Ben Jonson's *Works,* 1616). The decision to print the works of a popular playwright in folio is an indication of how far up on the social scale the theatrical profession had come during Shakespeare's lifetime. The Shakespeare folio was an expensive book, selling for between fifteen and eighteen shillings, depending on the binding (in modern terms, from about $150 to $180). Twenty Shakespeare plays of the thirty-seven that survive first appeared in quarto, seventeen of which appeared during Shakespeare's lifetime; the rest of the plays are found only in folio.

The First Folio was published in 1623, seven years after Shakespeare's death, and was authorized by his fellow actors, the co-owners of the King's Men. This publication was certainly a mark of the company's enormous respect for Shakespeare; but it was also a way of turning the old plays, most of which were no longer current in the playhouse, into ready money (the folio includes only Shakespeare's plays, not his sonnets or other nondramatic verse). Whatever the motives behind the publication of the folio, the texts it preserves constitute the basis for almost all later editions of the playwright's works. The texts, however, differ from those of the earlier quartos, sometimes in minor respects but often significantly – most strikingly in the two texts of *King Lear,* but also in important ways in *Hamlet, Othello,* and *Troilus and Cressida.* (The variants are recorded in the textual notes to each play in the new Pelican series.) The differences in these texts represent, in a sense, the essence of theater: the texts of plays were initially not intended for publication. They were scripts, designed for the actors to perform – the principal life of the play at this period was in performance. And it follows that in Shakespeare's theater the playwright typically had no say either in how his play was performed or in the disposition of his text – he was an employee of the company. The authoritative figures in the theatrical enterprise were the shareholders in the company, who were for the most part the major actors. They decided what plays were to be done; they hired the playwright and often gave him an outline of the play they wanted him to write. Often, too, the play was a collaboration: the company would retain a group of writers, and parcel out the scenes among them. The resulting script was then the property of the company, and the actors would revise it as they saw fit during the course of putting it on stage. The resulting text belonged to the company. The playwright had no rights in it once he had been paid. (This system survives largely intact in the movie industry, and most of the playwrights of Shakespeare's time were as anonymous as most screenwriters are today.) The script could also, of course, continue to change as the tastes of audiences and the requirements of the actors changed. Many – perhaps most – plays were revised when they were reintroduced after any substantial absence from the repertory, or when they were performed by a company different from the one that originally commissioned the play.

Shakespeare was an exceptional figure in this world because he was not only a shareholder and actor in his company, but also its leading playwright – he was literally his own boss. He had, moreover, little interest in the publication of his plays, and even those that appeared during his lifetime with the authorization of the company show no signs of any editorial concern on the part of the author. Theater was, for Shakespeare, a fluid and supremely responsive medium – the very opposite of the great classic canonical text that has embodied his works since 1623.

The very fluidity of the original texts, however, has meant that Shakespeare has always had to be edited. Here is an example of how problematic the editorial project inevitably is, a passage from the most famous speech in *Romeo and Juliet,* Juliet's balcony soliloquy beginning "O Romeo, Romeo, wherefore art thou Romeo?" Since the eighteenth century, the standard modern text has read,

> What's Montague? It is nor hand, nor foot,
> Nor arm, nor face, nor any other part
> Belonging to a man. O be some other name!
> What's in a name? That which we call a rose
> By any other name would smell as sweet.
>
> (II.2.40-44)

Editors have three early texts of this play to work from, two quarto texts and the folio. Here is how the First Quarto (1597) reads:

> Whats *Mountague?* It is nor hand nor foote,
> Nor arme,nor face, nor any other part.
> Whats in a name? That which we call a Rose,
> By any other name would smell as sweet:

Here is the Second Quarto (1599):

xxviii   THE TEXTS OF SHAKESPEARE

> Whats *Mountague*? it is nor hand nor foote,
> Nor arme nor face, ô be some other name
> Belonging to a man.
> Whats in a name that which we call a rose,
> By any other word would smell as sweete,

And here is the First Folio (1623):

> What's *Mountague*? it is nor hand nor foote,
> Nor arme, nor face, O be some other name
> Belonging to a man.
> What? in a names that which we call a Rose,
> By any other word would smell as sweete,

There is in fact no early text that reads as our modern text does – and this is the most famous speech in the play. Instead, we have three quite different texts, all of which are clearly some version of the same speech, but none of which seems to us a final or satisfactory version. The transcendently beautiful passage in modern editions is an editorial invention: editors have succeeded in conflating and revising the three versions into something we recognize as great poetry. Is this what Shakespeare "really" wrote? Who can say? What we can say is that Shakespeare always had performance, not a book, in mind.

Books About the Shakespeare Texts

The standard study of the printing history of the First Folio is W. W. Greg, *The Shakespeare First Folio* (1955). J. K. Walton, *The Quarto Copy for the First Folio of Shakespeare* (1971), is a useful survey of the relation of the quartos to the folio. The second edition of Charlton Hinman's *Norton Facsimile* of the First Folio (1996), with a new introduction by Peter Blayney, is indispensable. Stanley Wells, Gary Taylor, John Jowett, and William Montgomery, *William Shakespeare: A Textual Companion*, keyed to the Oxford text, gives a comprehensive survey of the editorial situation for all the plays and poems.

THE GENERAL EDITORS

Introduction

WHEN CLAUDIO BRUTALLY REJECTS Hero in public, just at the very moment that Friar Francis is about to marry them, it takes some time before his torrent of abuse turns to accusing her specifically of what Claudio believed he had seen the night before, the apparent conversation between Hero and Borachio at her window. In reply, Hero speaks a single line, a bald statement of denial: "I talked with no man at that hour, my lord" (IV.1.85). For Lewis Carroll, writing with characteristic impishness to Ellen Terry, whom he had seen playing Beatrice opposite Henry Irving as Benedick at the Lyceum Theatre in 1883, the statement was not enough:

> Why in the world did not Hero . . . prove an "alibi," in answer to the charge? It seems certain she did *not* sleep in her own room that night; for how could Margaret venture to open the window and talk from it, with her mistress asleep in the room? It would be sure to wake her. Besides, Borachio says . . . "I will so fashion the matter that Hero shall be absent" [II.2.42–43]. . . . Well, then, granting that Hero slept in some other room that night, why didn't she say so? When Claudio asks her, "What man was he talked with you yesternight out at your window betwixt twelve and one?" Why doesn't she reply: "I talked with no man at that hour, my lord. Nor was I in my chamber yesternight, but in another, far from it remote."

Carroll was, as he wrote, "only jesting" but Terry enjoyed his pointing out "slips in the dramatist's logic which only he would ever have noticed!" Shakespeare's plots can often creak, but in this case Carroll is being deliberately and delightfully unfair. At this appalling moment, Claudio, supported by the authority of Don Pedro, is more willing to believe his eyes than his ears, trusting to his misapprehension of the playacting put on for his benefit the night before rather than to Hero's assertion of absolute innocence. Mere verbal evidence would not convince him.

More striking than Shakespeare's refusal to end his drama prematurely is his refusal to stage the performance at the window itself, a lack that some theater directors and Kenneth Branagh in his 1993 film version have sought to repair. Shakespeare chose to do without a scene that had so often been a part of the narrative in the many versions that Shakespeare knew or might have encountered of the story of the virtuous woman falsely accused of unchastity. In one of Shakespeare's principal sources, for instance, Matteo Bandello's twenty-second tale in his *Novelle* (1554), Timbreo is deceived into thinking that Fenecia is meeting another lover by night when he sees a servant, dressed as a gentleman, climbing a ladder to a window in the house of Lionato, Fenecia's father. It seems especially significant to eliminate a scene so eminently dramatic in its games with role-playing and perception.

While Shakespeare took some names, the location of the action in Messina, and some parts of the narrative form from Bandello, he did not find there any example of what would become Margaret's impersonation of Hero at the window. That element of the action was available to him in Book 5 of Sir John Harington's 1591 translation of Ariosto's *Orlando Furioso,* where the maid Dalinda is persuaded by her lover to dress up as her mistress, Genevra, with the result that Genevra is rejected by Ariodante, who has seen the encounter. Genevra's clothes alone are enough to convince Ariodante that he has seen Genevra herself. Shakespeare's play is much concerned with clothes and fashion: Margaret's elaborate comparison of Hero's wedding gown with one worn by the Duchess of Milan (III.4.13–22) is the epitome of the trope. *Much Ado About*

Nothing is also anxious over the ways people fashion plots as Don Pedro "doubt[s] not but to fashion" a match between Beatrice and Benedick (II.1.347–48), and Borachio will "fashion" Hero's absence from her bedchamber (II.2.42–43). In the watchmen's mistakings "fashion" even becomes anthropomorphized into a "deformed thief" (III.3.124).

But clothes do not convince Claudio and Don Pedro. Instead, they believe they have seen Hero simply because of the location for the encounter and because they have heard Borachio "call Margaret Hero" (II.2.39–40). Editors and directors alike have had problems with Borachio's statement that the watchers will "hear Margaret term me Claudio" (40), and the line has often been emended to "call me Borachio." But it seems part of the viciousness of the scene that the audience is forced to imagine that "Hero" should have mockingly called her secret lover "Claudio" as part of their sex game. While Don John has made Claudio and Don Pedro voyeurs of the sexual encounter, Shakespeare controls the audience's sexual imaginings.

In the first scene of *Much Ado About Nothing* the prince and Claudio discuss another impersonation: Don Pedro will woo Hero at the "reveling," telling her "I am Claudio" (I.1.306). But it never occurs to Don Pedro and Claudio that someone else is capable of the same kind of trick. Having seen this conversation between Don Pedro and Claudio, the audience is given two accounts of it: the first, by Antonio to Leonato in I.2, is itself a retelling of the report Antonio has had from one of his servants; the second is recounted by Borachio to Don John in I.3. While Borachio relates the substance of the dialogue accurately (and productions have often brought Borachio on to eavesdrop in the first scene to show that he speaks the truth), Antonio's secondhand version turns it into a complete muddle.

While the play's title looks at first sight to be another of Shakespeare's disarming throwaways, like *As You Like It* or the alternative title for *Twelfth Night*, *What You Will*, it is also a complex punning on its last word. "Nothing" could be pronounced "noting" in early modern English, and the play is clearly fascinated by what people note when they eavesdrop others' conversations. From the false conversations that lead Benedick and Beatrice to believe that each is in love with the other to the consequences of the mis-hearings or misunderstandings of Antonio's man, the play develops much of its action out of this pun on its title. The audience is not permitted to note the crucial act of mis-"noting," the window scene. It too must rely on report, on accounts of what was seen. The spectators cannot help imagining and perhaps overelaborating the images that are conjured up, making much of what may have been nothing.

But "nothing," which Hamlet described as "a fair thought to lie between maids' legs" (III.2.14), was also, for Shakespeare's contemporaries, a contemptuous male term for female genitals and, in that light, the pun in the title appears to be pointing to the extraordinary and excessive fuss that men make over the object of their sexual desire and over their obsession with female chastity. In the disguisings of the dance in II.1 – another moment when the male characters take on and deny other identities while the women stay unmasked and undisguised – there are further opportunities for mistakes about noting and nothing as the dancers pair off into couples where the male interest might well be in the objectification of women as merely a female nothing.

In this world, it is disturbingly easy for Don John and Borachio to convince Claudio that the conversation between Don Pedro and Hero has shown the prince wooing for himself. In effect Don John and Borachio pretend that Antonio's false account of the dialogue between Don Pedro and Claudio has proved true, playing on the misunderstanding under which all of Leonato's family has been laboring, believing that Don Pedro wished to marry Hero himself. When Hero chats wittily with Don Pedro as they take a turn in the dance, she must have expected the prince to be about to offer to marry her himself and she shows herself signally indifferent as to whether she is to marry Don Pedro or Claudio. She is, in effect, far more willing to say "Father, as it please you" than "Father, as it please me" (II.1.50-52).

All the sources and analogues that Shakespeare could have known made the assumption of the woman's unchastity the product of the machinations of a rival lover, usually someone who is a close friend of the man who is being deceived (in Bandello, for instance, it had been Timbreo's friend Girondo). It is as if, in Don Pedro's wooing Hero, the play is toying with the possibility of such an action, such a disruption of male comradeship and friendship between the victors in the recent battle, before resolving it within the same scene and clearing the way for a more dangerous antithesis.

For Coleridge, as he recorded in notes probably made in 1813, *Much Ado About Nothing* was proof that in Shakespeare "the plot interests us on account of the characters, not vice versa; it is the canvas only":

> Take away from *Much Ado About Nothing* all that which is not indispensable to the plot, either as having little to do with it, or at best, like Dogberry and his comrades, forced into the service when any other less ingeniously absurd watchmen and night-constables would have answered; take away Benedick, Beatrice, Dogberry, and the reaction of the former on the character of Hero, and what will remain? In other writers the main agent of the plot is always the prominent character. In Shakespeare so or not so, as the character is in itself calculated or not calculated to form the plot. So Don John, the mainspring of the plot, is merely shown and withdrawn.

For Ursula, when she tells Beatrice the good news that the truth has come out, Don John was "the author of all"

(V.2.92), but for Borachio, when he faces the father of the woman whom he killed "with thy breath," he carries sole responsibility: "Yea, even I alone" (V.1.255). To Ursula it appears that "the prince and Claudio [are] mightily abused" (V.2.91-92), but to Leonato this "pair of honorable men – / A third is fled – that had a hand in it" (V.1.257-58) shares the blame equally with Don John. Coleridge is accurate in his assessment of Don John as "mainspring," as a plot mechanism that winds up the action and keeps it going, but Don John needs more accomplices than Conrad and Borachio. Don Pedro and Claudio prove to be easy dupes.

Taciturn and opaque – and for most actors almost unplayable – Don John epitomizes a villainy that, for the other characters and some critics, it is too easy to see as external to the community of Messina and its guests. But at the play's opening the civilian town welcomes back soldiers returning from war, and many productions keep Don Pedro and others in military uniform, a prolonged reminder of the antagonism between brothers that was the war's cause. It has been a bloodless war, at least as far as the aristocracy is concerned, a battle in which the losses have been only among the common soldiers ("none of name," I.1.7), a mark of the play's examination of aristocratic codes of behavior. But Don John's manner, from his first appearance brooding and, but for a single line, silent (like Hero), hints at the uneasiness of the reconciliation between the brothers.

Though the stage direction for Don John's first entry identifies him as "John the Bastard" (I.1.89 s.d.), it is not until Benedick voices his suspicions after the rejection of Hero that the dialogue tells the audience that Don John's unconventional parentage marks him with the attribute of the conventional villain: "The practice of it lives in John the Bastard" (IV.1.188). Socially excluded from power that is vested, as Edmund complains in *King Lear,* in the legitimate offspring, Don John appears to be – and seems to construct himself as being – socially marginalized. But his isolation is something he shares with his half brother. For, at the end of the play, Don Pedro can appear onstage conspicuously alone. It may be practicable for Benedick not to think about the captured Don John "till tomorrow" (V.4.125) but Don Pedro may not be able to share the willingness to postpone dealing with his brother.

Don Pedro is also excluded from the matrimonial couplings that end the play. Benedick, speaking with a striking lack of social deference, may call on him to "Get thee a wife" (120) but there is no one for Don Pedro to marry. Exactly why Don Pedro should offer to woo Hero on Claudio's behalf can be unclear. It may make sense for the prince to discuss the terms of marriage with Hero's father but his intervention in the wooing itself, ventriloquizing Claudio, leaves a curious suggestion of a sexual game, a piece of erotic role-playing that is much more than Don Pedro's earlier offer to "break with her." Don Pedro's "amorous tale" (I.1.309) is clearly intended to stimulate Hero sexually as if, without it, a demure – and to this point noticeably silent – young woman like Hero could not possibly be thinking about marriage and that marriage cannot be thought about without making much ado about sex. But when he announces that "in her bosom I'll unclasp my heart" (307) the audience might wonder what vicarious satisfaction the impersonation offers Don Pedro. In the sources for the Hero plot there had usually been a conspicuous gap of social status between the woman and the lover who accuses her. Shakespeare narrows the gap: Claudio is a count, Hero the daughter of the governor of Messina. But Don Pedro's interest in pretending to be Claudio suggests a patronizing abuse of power. Claudio's readiness to believe Don John's account of the prince wooing for himself may not be entirely a matter of Claudio's gullibility.

In the conversation that follows the betrothal of Claudio and Hero in II.1, Don Pedro asks Beatrice, "Will you have me, lady?" (308). In performance, Beatrice's "No, my lord" has been played as a lighthearted rejection of a genuine proposal of marriage but it is a snub that Don Pedro can find deeply hurtful. The plot to bring Beatrice and Benedick together that Don Pedro outlines soon after can therefore seem Don Pedro's revenge on Beatrice for her unthinking dismissal of his offer. The words of Balthasar's song, "Men were deceivers ever" (II.3.61), has often been used in productions to stand overemphatically as the play's meaning: we hear it at the beginning and end of Kenneth Branagh's film as well as at the point in the action prescribed by Shakespeare. Don Pedro, as much as his half brother, is a deceiver.

If the song warns women of male deception, the play also manifests the risk to other men. Male friendship, whether viewed as camaraderie or as a revelation of homoerotic desire, is always at risk in the play. Even at the end, there seems less difficulty in bringing Beatrice and Benedick together than in bringing about a reconciliation between Benedick and Claudio, who are still trading insults and threats a few lines from the play's close. Don Pedro and Claudio, in particular, close male ranks with frightening ease after the apparent death of Hero. Nothing Claudio does is as callous as his description of the impotent threats from the grieving Leonato and Antonio: "We had liked to have had our two noses snapped off with two old men without teeth" (V.1.115-16). His question to Don Pedro, "Hath Leonato any son?" (I.1.278), may be justifiable caution to ensure that Hero is indeed Leonato's "only heir." Even the shaming of Hero at the altar has some social justification, since immorality between the contract and the marriage was one of the few grounds sufficient to annul a contract, and only a public statement would be a way of protecting the wronged bridegroom from a subsequent accusation of marriage-breaking. But Hero's presumed unchastity does not warrant this treatment of Leonato, and Claudio's charmless comment is echoed by Don Pedro's apparently unconcerned ease in making passing reference, as he mocks

Benedick, to the "old man's daughter" (V.1.173), the "dead" Hero.

The friar's hope that feigning Hero's death will make Claudio mourn "And wish he had not so accusèd her" (IV.1.232) clearly does not work and we are left to wonder whether this failure does not prove that love never "had interest in his liver" (IV.1.231). The audience is also left to wonder why the "resurrected" Hero should be so willing to marry the young man, scarcely more than a boy, who has so completely failed to prove his love. After Claudio has done penance at Hero's "tomb," Don Pedro offers an exquisite quatrain describing the dawn, but his lines include an unwitting pun that throws a harsh judgment back on himself and on Claudio. Night's threats are signaled in his comment that the "wolves have preyed" (V.3.25), but the audience cannot help but hear as a homophone that Don Pedro and Claudio are the wolves who have prayed.

In their plotting Don Pedro and Claudio have already shown their attitude toward their supposed friendship with Benedick. Though the outcome of the trick, which has been offered as an impossibly Herculean labor (II.1.344-47) simply to fill up the time between betrothal and marriage, is to bring together two people who the audience must feel deserve each other in such profound ways, the gulling is set up as another part of Don Pedro's self-regarding authority. Beatrice has already told the prince that there was a previous relationship between Benedick and herself but that he abandoned it: "he lent it [i.e., his heart] me awhile, and I gave him use for it – a double heart for his single one. Marry, once before he won it of me with false dice; therefore your grace may well say I have lost it" (II.1.263-66). Don Pedro's trick is designed to force back together two people whose previous attempt at love had foundered on male deception. It will take courage for Beatrice, in particular, to be prepared to commit herself again to a man who had treated her in this fashion.

As so often, Beatrice's witty response, describing their past, suggests considerable pain behind it. Even Don Pedro's compliment that she was born "in a merry hour" only leads her to point out that "sure, . . . my mother cried" (II.1.316). Beatrice occupies a difficult social position in Leonato's household as an unmarried and orphaned woman. She compensates for it both by refusing to be a silent member of the family and by the sharp brilliance of her language, which so completely overshadows her quiet cousin Hero. Beatrice denies her own social marginalization. But Hero's account of Beatrice when Beatrice is fooled into believing Benedick is in love with her is in marked contrast with the men's description of Benedick at the parallel moment. Where, Don Pedro's comment on Benedick's "contemptible spirit" (II.3.175) aside, the men praise Benedick, albeit mockingly, Hero's lines on Beatrice's "Disdain and scorn" have an altogether harsher edge (III.1.51-56):

> She cannot love,
> Nor take no shape nor project of affection,
> She is so self-endeared.

It sounds uncomfortably like Hero's taking the opportunity to pay back Beatrice for the latter's powerful position in Hero's father's home.

The action of almost everyone in Messina, apart from Beatrice and Benedick, can appear at best mean-spirited (and at worst, downright vicious). But, as Coleridge's comment (quoted above) recognizes, these two stand apart from the main plot. Indeed this play, which is so much theirs that it is no surprise that Charles I wrote their names opposite the title in his copy of the Second Folio, hardly needs them for its crucial action to be accomplished. Shakespeare seems to have had no particular source for these witty lovers, though they have had a myriad progeny, standing as the prototype for so many cautious, worldly-wise, witty couples in Restoration comedy and thereafter. The one significant action that Beatrice tries to engage Benedick in, killing Claudio, is one he initially turns down, "not for the wide world" (IV.1.289). Benedick refuses to ride to the rescue like a romance hero, ready to do his mistress's bidding the moment it is uttered. Instead he has to test out the depth of her rational conviction that Claudio has been wrong. It takes nearly forty lines and Beatrice's crying three times over "O that I were a man" until she has answered with the most absolute assuredness his question, "Think you in your soul the Count Claudio hath wronged Hero?" (326-27), before Benedick can say abruptly, "Enough, I am engaged" (329). Benedick is finally prepared to value his love of Beatrice and her judgment on Claudio. But he is also prepared to leave his own reputation to hearsay and rumor: "As you hear of me, so think of me" (331-32), a remarkable willingness in a play in which almost all report proves untrue.

Most audiences find Beatrice's command "Kill Claudio" unnerving. Though, among Shakespeare's sources for the plot, Bandello's and Ariosto's stories both ended happily, like numerous other versions of the action (for example, the play *Fedele and Fortunio,* probably written by Anthony Munday in 1585), Shakespeare probably also knew Spenser's dark retelling in *The Faerie Queene* (1590), where the Claudio figure (Philemon) kills his falsely accused Hero (Claribell). From the messenger's account of the war onward, death has hovered on the margins of the narrative, continually threatening to take center stage. Borachio had told Don John that the proof of Hero's unchastity would be enough to "kill Leonato" (II.2.27) but Leonato has proved more likely to kill Hero than himself, more concerned to save the family honor by her death than by his own. Hero will be reported dead but she will be dead only "whiles her slander lived" (V.4.66). Beatrice's command brings death into the active space of the male world, and its announcement, hard on the heels of Beatrice's and Benedick's tentative expression of their love, is a frighteningly abrupt shift of register, often enough in performance to produce uneasy laughter, which the actor playing Beatrice usually works hard to kill. The tonal uncertainty that provokes the audience response can make killing the laugh as difficult as any other kind of death in the play.

It proves in the world of Messina not to be enough simply to be witty, dazzlingly witty though Beatrice and Benedick may be. Benedick must, for his love, wear his wit in his scabbard (V.1.125). He must abandon the service of Don Pedro. He must endure his former comrades' gibes and turn his own language into a more direct tool, no longer epigrammatic but threatening:

> You are a villain. I jest not; I will make it good how
> you dare, with what you dare, and when you dare.
> Do me right, or I will protest your cowardice. You
> have killed a sweet lady, and her death shall fall
> heavy on you. Let me hear from you.
>
> (143-47)

This stream of plain speaking, with its simple syntax and simpler vocabulary – forty-six of the fifty-one words of the speech are monosyllables – is unrecognizable as the language of the earlier Benedick. Comparison with a characteristic speech in the first scene of the play shows the distance he has gone:

> That a woman conceived me, I thank her; that she
> brought me up, I likewise give her most humble
> thanks; but that I will have a recheat winded in my
> forehead, or hang my bugle in an invisible baldrick,
> all women shall pardon me.
>
> (227-31)

He may be no poet, unable to find rhymes for his verse (V.2.35-39), but the transformation to the seriousness of a committed lover is more profound than an adept use of the language of love poetry would ever have indicated.

Beatrice and Benedick enjoy language and are – usually – easy in their control. The value they place on their linguistic dexterity is part of their defense against the threatening world around them. The watchmen may be inept; their leader, Dogberry, may, like so many of Shakespeare's clowns, mistake language as, striving for sophistication, he invents nonexistent words. But, as Borachio tells Don Pedro and Claudio, "What your wisdoms could not discover, these shallow fools have brought to light" (V.1.224-26). It is part of the brilliance of Shakespeare's plotting that, if Leonato had been prepared to listen a little longer to the ado that Dogberry was making much of in III.5, the rejection of Hero would never have occurred. It is easy to laugh at Dogberry, but he sees himself as a man with dignity, horrified that "a householder . . . that knows the law," let alone "a fellow that hath had losses; and one that hath two gowns and everything handsome about him," should have been called "an ass" (IV.2.79-84).

In the general rejoicings at the end of the play even Margaret can be forgiven her part in the catastrophe, her ignorance a sufficient defense. But the audience may be left to wonder whether Dogberry is really the ass of the play, whether even those who are gulled like Beatrice and Benedick may not be less foolish than those who so firmly believed themselves to be wise. Though deceived and mocked by friends and family, Beatrice and Benedick prove that they know exactly what it is worth making much ado about and that what they value is worth far more than nothing.

PETER HOLLAND
The Shakespeare Institute,
The University of Birmingham

Note on the Text

THE PRESENT EDITION follows closely the text of the only quarto of the play, that printed in 1600, evidently from Shakespeare's own draft. It is an excellent text despite irregularities in the speech and scene headings, which are unusually numerous and may reflect indecisions and slight changes of plan during the process of composition. The names of the actors Will Kemp and Richard Cowley prefixing the speeches of Dogberry and Verges in IV.2 indicate that the manuscript was closely related to the first stage production; however, the irregularities mentioned above would presumably have been eliminated if the manuscript had served as promptbook. The quarto text is not divided into acts and scenes, and the text in the folio, which was printed from it, is divided into acts but not into scenes. The division supplied for reference in the present edition is that of later editors, who divided the folio acts into scenes.

Below are listed all substantive departures from the quarto of 1600, with the adopted reading in italics followed by the quarto reading in roman. The need for emendation is remarkably slight, and most of the following instances involve mere normalization of stage directions and speech prefixes. They are listed because of the theatrical interest of some of them. Most of the irregularities are repeated in the folio text of 1623, which was printed from the quarto and is of little value in forming the text. However, two of the folio stage directions have some slight theatrical interest. The folio adds to the stage direction at II.1.79: "Maskers with a drum"; and gives as the stage direction at II.3.34 "Enter Prince, Leonato, Claudio, and Iacke Wilson," indicating that in some performance before 1623 the singer John Wilson played the part of Balthasar.

I.1 s.d. *Messina, Hero* Messina, Innogen his wife, Hero   **8** *Pedro* Peter   **193 s.d.** *Enter Don Pedro* (Q adds: Iohn the bastard)

I.2 3, 6, 16 *ANTONIO* Old   **6** *event* euents   **24** *skill* shill

I.3 s.d. *[Don]* Sir   **43** *brother's* bothers

II.1 s.d. *brother* brother, his wife; *niece* neece, and a kinsman   **2, 18, 47** *ANTONIO* brother   **79 s.d.** *Prince [Don] Pedro* prince, Pedro; *Don John* or dumb Iohn   **80** *a bout* about   **94, 97, 99** *BALTHASAR* Bene.   **199 s.d.** *Prince* Prince, Hero, Leonato, Iohn and Borachio, and Conrade   **307** *PEDRO* Prince (thus throughout scene except l. 329: Pedro)

II.3 7 s.d. *Exit* (at l. 5 in Q)   **24** *an* and   **34 s.d.** (Q adds "Musicke")   **35** *PEDRO* Prince (thus throughout)   **60** *BALTHASAR* (not in Q)   **64-65** *Then . . . go* (single line in Q)   **87 s.d.** *Exit Balthasar* (occurs after l. 86 in Q)   **132** *us of* of vs   **232 s.d.** *Enter Beatrice* (after l. 233 in Q)

III.1 23 s.d. *Enter Beatrice* (occurs after l. 25 in Q)

III.2 1 *PEDRO* Prince (thus throughout except at l. 50: Bene.)   **26** *can* cannot   **72** *JOHN* Bastard (thus throughout)   **103** *her then* her, then

III.3 11 *FIRST WATCHMAN* Watch I   **17, 28** *SECOND WATCHMAN* Watch 2   **38** *A WATCHMAN* Watch (thus thereafter until ll. 162 ff., where "Watch I" and "Watch 2" are resumed)   **173-74** *Never . . . us* (part of preceding speech by Conrad in Q)

III.4 17 *in* it

III.5 2 *DOGBERRY* Const. Dog. (thus throughout except ll. 54, 58)   **7** *VERGES* Headb. (thus throughout except l. 57)   **9** *off* of   **49** *be suffigance* (Q adds Exit)

IV.1 4 *FRIAR* Fran.   **28, 62, 86** *PEDRO* Prince   **49-50** *And . . . Leonato* (single line in Q)   **66, 110** *JOHN* Bastard   **155-58** *Hear . . . marked* (printed as prose in Q, crowded at foot of page)

IV.2 s.d. *Enter . . . Watch* (Q reads "Enter the Constables, Borachio, and the Towne clearke in gownes")   **1** *DOGBERRY* Keeper   **2, 5** *VERGES* Cowley   **4** *DOGBERRY* Andrew   **9** *DOGBERRY* Kemp (thus or variants throughout except l. 65: Constable)   **37, 51** *FIRST WATCHMAN* Watch 1   **45** *SECOND WATCHMAN* Watch. 2   **49** *VERGES* Const.   **57** *WATCHMEN* Watch   **66** *VERGES* Couley   **66-67** *hands – /CONRAD Off, coxcomb!* hands of Coxcombe   **71** *CONRAD* Couley

V.1 1 *ANTONIO* Brother (thus throughout)   **16** *Bid* And   **96** *an* (not in Q)   **97** *off* of   **109 s.d.** *Exeunt ambo* (occurs at l. 108 in Q)   **200** *DOGBERRY* Const. (thus throughout)   **248** *VERGES* Con. 2

V.2 26-29 *The . . . deserve* (printed as prose in Q)   **41 s.d.** *Enter Beatrice* (occurs after l. 42 in Q)   **46** *for* (omitted in Q)

V.3 3 *CLAUDIO* (appears at l. 11 in Q)   **10** *dumb* dead   **22** *CLAUDIO* Lo.   **22-23** *Now . . . rite* (single line in Q)   **24, 30** *PEDRO* Prince

V.4 7, 17 *ANTONIO* Old   **34** *PEDRO* Prince (thus throughout except at l. 40: P.)   **97** *Benedick* Leon.

Much Ado About Nothing

[Names of the Actors

DON PEDRO, *Prince of Aragon*
BENEDICK, *of Padua* } *lords attending on Don*
CLAUDIO, *of Florence* } *Pedro*

BALTHASAR, *a singer, attending on Don Pedro*
A BOY, *serving Benedick*
DON JOHN, *the bastard brother of Don Pedro*
BORACHIO } *followers of Don John*
CONRAD }
LEONATO, *Governor of Messina*
HERO, *his daughter*
BEATRICE, *his niece*
ANTONIO, *an old man, Leonato's brother*
MARGARET } *waiting gentlewomen, attending on Hero*
URSULA }
FRIAR FRANCIS
DOGBERRY, *the constable in charge of the watch*
VERGES, *the headborough*
A SEXTON
WATCHMEN (*including George Seacoal*)
ATTENDANTS, MESSENGERS, MUSICIANS

SCENE: *Messina*]
*

Much Ado About Nothing

∾ I.1 *Enter Leonato, Governor of Messina, Hero his
daughter, and Beatrice his niece, with a Messenger.*

LEONATO I learn in this letter that Don Pedro of Aragon
comes this night to Messina.

MESSENGER He is very near by this. He was not three
leagues off when I left him.

LEONATO How many gentlemen have you lost in this
action? 6

MESSENGER But few of any sort, and none of name. 7

LEONATO A victory is twice itself when the achiever
brings home full numbers. I find here that Don Pedro
hath bestowed much honor on a young Florentine 10
called Claudio.

MESSENGER Much deserved on his part, and equally
remembered by Don Pedro. He hath borne himself be- 13
yond the promise of his age, doing in the figure of a
lamb the feats of a lion. He hath indeed better bettered
expectation than you must expect of me to tell you how.

LEONATO He hath an uncle here in Messina will be very
much glad of it.

MESSENGER I have already delivered him letters, and
there appears much joy in him, even so much that joy 20

I.1 Messina s.d. (Q includes here, and at the opening of II.1, an entry for
"Innogen," Leonato's wife; editors have assumed from the fact that she never
speaks and her absence from her daughter's wedding that she was an early
thought of Shakespeare's, subsequently incompletely dropped. But she could
be played onstage, even in the shadowy form Q offers.) **6** *action* battle **7**
sort rank; *name* importance **13** *remembered* rewarded

21 could not show itself modest enough without a badge
    of bitterness.

    LEONATO   Did he break out into tears?

    MESSENGER   In great measure.

25 LEONATO   A kind overflow of kindness. There are no
    faces truer than those that are so washed. How much
    better is it to weep at joy than to joy at weeping!

28 BEATRICE   I pray you, is Signor Montanto returned from
    the wars or no?

30 MESSENGER   I know none of that name, lady. There was
    none such in the army of any sort.

    LEONATO   What is he that you ask for, niece?

33 HERO   My cousin means Signor Benedick of Padua.

    MESSENGER   O, he's returned, and as pleasant as ever he
    was.

36 BEATRICE   He set up his bills here in Messina and chal-
37 lenged Cupid at the flight, and my uncle's fool, reading
38 the challenge, subscribed for Cupid and challenged
39 him at the bird bolt. I pray you, how many hath he
40 killed and eaten in these wars? But how many hath he
    killed? For indeed I promised to eat all of his killing.

42 LEONATO   Faith, niece, you tax Signor Benedick too
43 much, but he'll be meet with you, I doubt it not.

    MESSENGER   He hath done good service, lady, in these
    wars.

46 BEATRICE   You had musty victual, and he hath holp to
47 eat it. He is a very valiant trencherman, he hath an ex-
48 cellent stomach.

    MESSENGER   And a good soldier too, lady.

---

21 *modest* moderate   21–22 *badge of bitterness* i.e., tears   25 *kind* natural
28 *Montanto* montanto, an upward thrust in fencing (suggesting a social
climber and someone who "mounts" sexually)   33 *Benedick* (from Latin
benedictus, blessed)   36 *set up his bills* posted advertisements   37 *at the
flight* to an archery duel; *my uncle's fool* (possibly Beatrice herself)   38 *subscribed* signed (as Cupid's representative)   39 *bird bolt* small blunt arrow al-
lowed to boys as harmless, but also Cupid's arrow   42 *tax* criticize   43 *meet*
even   46 *musty victual* stale provisions; *holp* helped   47 *trencherman* eater
48 *stomach* appetite

BEATRICE   And a good soldier to a lady, but what is he to   50
a lord?

MESSENGER   A lord to a lord, a man to a man, stuffed   52
with all honorable virtues.

BEATRICE   It is so indeed. He is no less than a stuffed   54
man; but for the stuffing – well, we are all mortal.

LEONATO   You must not, sir, mistake my niece. There is a
kind of merry war betwixt Signor Benedick and her.
They never meet but there's a skirmish of wit between
them.

BEATRICE   Alas, he gets nothing by that! In our last con-   60
flict four of his five wits went halting off, and now is   61
the whole man governed with one, so that if he have
wit enough to keep himself warm, let him bear it for a   63
difference between himself and his horse, for it is all the   64
wealth that he hath left to be known a reasonable crea-   65
ture. Who is his companion now? He hath every
month a new sworn brother.

MESSENGER   Is't possible?

BEATRICE   Very easily possible. He wears his faith but as   69
the fashion of his hat: it ever changes with the next   70
block.   71

MESSENGER   I see, lady, the gentleman is not in your
books.   73

BEATRICE   No. An he were, I would burn my study. But I   74
pray you, who is his companion? Is there no young
squarer now that will make a voyage with him to the   76
devil?

MESSENGER   He is most in the company of the right
noble Claudio.

BEATRICE   O Lord, he will hang upon him like a disease!   80
He is sooner caught than the pestilence, and the taker   81

---

50 *to* in comparison with   52 *stuffed* supplied   54 *stuffed man* figure stuffed
to look like a man   61 *five wits* mental faculties; *halting* limping   63 *bear*
show (in his coat of arms)   64 *difference* distinguishing mark (heraldic term)
65 *reasonable* capable of reasoning   69 *faith* truth to his oath   71 *block* hat
block – i.e., style   73 *books* favor   74 *An* if   76 *squarer* quarreler   80 *he*
i.e., Benedick   81 *pestilence* plague; *taker* infected person

82 runs presently mad. God help the noble Claudio! If he
have caught the Benedick, it will cost him a thousand
84 pound ere a be cured.
85 MESSENGER   I will hold friends with you, lady.
BEATRICE   Do, good friend.
87 LEONATO   You will never run mad, niece.
BEATRICE   No, not till a hot January.
MESSENGER   Don Pedro is approached.
*Enter Don Pedro, Claudio, Benedick, Balthasar, and
[Don] John the Bastard.*
90 PEDRO   Good Signor Leonato, are you come to meet
91 your trouble? The fashion of the world is to avoid cost,
92 and you encounter it.
LEONATO   Never came trouble to my house in the likeness of your grace, for trouble being gone, comfort
should remain, but when you depart from me, sorrow
abides and happiness takes his leave.
97 PEDRO   You embrace your charge too willingly. I think
this is your daughter.
LEONATO   Her mother hath many times told me so.
100 BENEDICK   Were you in doubt, sir, that you asked her?
LEONATO   Signor Benedick, no, for then were you a
child.
103 PEDRO   You have it full, Benedick. We may guess by this
104 what you are, being a man. Truly the lady fathers herself. Be happy, lady, for you are like an honorable
father.
BENEDICK   If Signor Leonato be her father, she would
108 not have his head on her shoulders for all Messina, as
like him as she is.
110 BEATRICE   I wonder that you will still be talking, Signor
111 Benedick. Nobody marks you.

---

82 *presently* immediately   **84** *a* he   **85** *hold* remain   **87** *run mad* i.e., "catch
the Benedick"   **91** *your trouble* the trouble of entertaining a noble guest   **92**
encounter go to meet   **97** *charge* expense, but also responsibility   **103** *have
it full* are fully answered   **104–5** *fathers herself* resembles and so indicates her
father   **108** *his head* (with its white hair and beard)   **111** *marks* notices

BENEDICK   What, my dear Lady Disdain! Are you yet
living?

BEATRICE   Is it possible disdain should die while she hath
such meet food to feed it as Signor Benedick? Courtesy   115
itself must convert to disdain if you come in her pres-   116
ence.

BENEDICK   Then is courtesy a turncoat. But it is certain I
am loved of all ladies, only you excepted, and I would I
could find in my heart that I had not a hard heart, for   120
truly I love none.

BEATRICE   A dear happiness to women! They would else   122
have been troubled with a pernicious suitor. I thank
God and my cold blood, I am of your humor for that. I   124
had rather hear my dog bark at a crow than a man
swear he loves me.

BENEDICK   God keep your ladyship still in that mind! So
some gentleman or other shall scape a predestinate   128
scratched face.

BEATRICE   Scratching could not make it worse an 'twere   130
such a face as yours were.

BENEDICK   Well, you are a rare parrot teacher.   132

BEATRICE   A bird of my tongue is better than a beast of   133
yours.

BENEDICK   I would my horse had the speed of your
tongue, and so good a continuer. But keep your way, a   136
God's name! I have done.

BEATRICE   You always end with a jade's trick. I know you   138
of old.

PEDRO   That is the sum of all, Leonato. Signor Claudio   140
and Signor Benedick, my dear friend Leonato hath in-

---

115 *meet* suitable   116 *convert* change   122 *dear* great   124 *humor for that*
opinion on that point   128 *predestinate* predestined, inevitable   132 *rare*
exceptional; *parrot teacher* one who teaches a parrot by repeating monoto-
nously   133 *A bird of my tongue* a bird that speaks   133–34 *a beast of yours*
a dumb beast   136 *continuer* one having endurance   138 *a jade's trick* stop-
ping suddenly (in this race of wit) like a recalcitrant horse   140 *sum of all*
whole account (of the recent campaign? Don Pedro and Leonato have been
talking apart)

vited you all. I tell him we shall stay here at the least a
month, and he heartily prays some occasion may detain
us longer. I dare swear he is no hypocrite, but prays
from his heart.

LEONATO If you swear, my lord, you shall not be
147   forsworn. *[To Don John]* Let me bid you welcome, my
148   lord. Being reconciled to the prince your brother, I owe
         you all duty.

150 JOHN   I thank you. I am not of many words, but I thank
         you.

LEONATO *[To Don Pedro]* Please it your grace lead on?

153 PEDRO   Your hand, Leonato. We will go together.

                    Exeunt. Manent Benedick and Claudio.

CLAUDIO Benedick, didst thou note the daughter of
         Signor Leonato?

156 BENEDICK I noted her not, but I looked on her.

CLAUDIO Is she not a modest young lady?

BENEDICK Do you question me as an honest man should
         do, for my simple true judgment? or would you have me
160   speak after my custom, as being a professed tyrant to
         their sex?

CLAUDIO No, I pray thee speak in sober judgment.

163 BENEDICK Why, i' faith, methinks she's too low for a
         high praise, too brown for a fair praise, and too little for
         a great praise. Only this commendation I can afford
         her, that were she other than she is, she were unhand-
         some, and being no other but as she is, I do not like
         her.

CLAUDIO Thou thinkest I am in sport. I pray thee tell
170   me truly how thou lik'st her.

BENEDICK Would you buy her, that you inquire after
         her?

CLAUDIO Can the world buy such a jewel?

---

147 *forsworn* proved a liar 148 *Being* since you are 153 *go together* (the
prince refuses to take precedence of his host); **s.d.** *Manent* remain 156
noted noticed especially 160 *tyrant to* railer against, detractor of 163 *low*
short

BENEDICK   Yea, and a case to put it into. But speak you   174
    this with a sad brow? or do you play the flouting jack, to   175
    tell us Cupid is a good hare finder and Vulcan a rare car-   176
    penter? Come, in what key shall a man take you to go in   177
    the song?

CLAUDIO   In mine eye she is the sweetest lady that ever I
    looked on.   *180*

BENEDICK   I can see yet without spectacles, and I see no
    such matter. There's her cousin, an she were not pos-
    sessed with a fury, exceeds her as much in beauty as the
    first of May doth the last of December. But I hope you
    have no intent to turn husband, have you?

CLAUDIO   I would scarce trust myself, though I had
    sworn the contrary, if Hero would be my wife.

BENEDICK   Is't come to this? In faith, hath not the world
    one man but he will wear his cap with suspicion? Shall   189
    I never see a bachelor of threescore again? Go to, i'   190
    faith, an thou wilt needs thrust thy neck into a yoke,
    wear the print of it and sigh away Sundays. Look! Don   192
    Pedro is returned to seek you.

    Enter Don Pedro.

PEDRO   What secret hath held you here, that you fol-
    lowed not to Leonato's?

BENEDICK   I would your grace would constrain me to   196
    tell.

PEDRO   I charge thee on thy allegiance.   198

BENEDICK   You hear, Count Claudio. I can be secret as a
    dumb man, I would have you think so, but, on my al-   *200*
    legiance – mark you this – on my allegiance! He is in

---

174 *case* (1) jewel case, (2) clothing, (3) vagina ("it" would then mean
"penis")   **175** *sad brow* serious mind; *flouting jack* mocking fellow   **176–77**
hare finder . . . carpenter (Cupid was blind and therefore hopeless at spotting
hares in the field; Vulcan, a blacksmith)   **177** *go* join   **189** *with suspicion* for
fear he has grown horns (i.e., been made a cuckold by an unfaithful wife)
190 *Go to* go on   **192** *sigh away Sundays* i.e., become a good "Sunday citi-
zen," a responsible and sober married man   **196** *constrain* force   **198** *allegiance* loyalty to me as your prince

202 love. With who? Now that is your grace's part. Mark
how short his answer is: with Hero, Leonato's short
daughter.

205 CLAUDIO If this were so, so were it uttered.

206 BENEDICK Like the old tale, my lord: "It is not so, nor
'twas not so, but indeed, God forbid it should be so!"

CLAUDIO If my passion change not shortly, God forbid
it should be otherwise.

210 PEDRO Amen, if you love her, for the lady is very well
worthy.

212 CLAUDIO You speak this to fetch me in, my lord.

PEDRO By my troth, I speak my thought.

CLAUDIO And, in faith, my lord, I spoke mine.

215 BENEDICK And, by my two faiths and troths, my lord, I
spoke mine.

CLAUDIO That I love her, I feel.

PEDRO That she is worthy, I know.

BENEDICK That I neither feel how she should be loved,
220 nor know how she should be worthy, is the opinion
221 that fire cannot melt out of me. I will die in it at the
stake.

223 PEDRO Thou wast ever an obstinate heretic in the despite of beauty.

225 CLAUDIO And never could maintain his part but in the
force of his will.

BENEDICK That a woman conceived me, I thank her;
that she brought me up, I likewise give her most hum-
229 ble thanks; but that I will have a recheat winded in my

---

202 *part* speech, in the theatrical sense 205 *so were it uttered* so would he
tell it 206 *old tale* (a version of the Bluebeard story in which the heroine's
report of her discoveries is punctuated by these words of protest from the
murderer) 212 *fetch me in* trick me 215 *two faiths and troths* one to each
(but also double-dealing is implied) 221 *fire . . . me* i.e., he will die at the
stake for his opinion 223–24 *in the despite* in showing scorn 225–26
maintain . . . will win the argument except by stubborn refusal to give in
(punning on "maintain his erection" and "will" as "sexual desire") 229
recheat series of notes on a horn sounded to call the hounds together (with
the usual reference to the cuckold's horns)

forehead, or hang my bugle in an invisible baldrick, all   230
women shall pardon me. Because I will not do them
the wrong to mistrust any, I will do myself the right to
trust none; and the fine is (for the which I may go the   233
finer), I will live a bachelor.   234

PEDRO   I shall see thee, ere I die, look pale with love.

BENEDICK   With anger, with sickness, or with hunger,
my lord, not with love. Prove that ever I lose more   237
blood with love than I will get again with drinking,
pick out mine eyes with a ballad-maker's pen and hang   239
me up at the door of a brothel house for the sign of   240
blind Cupid.

PEDRO   Well, if ever thou dost fall from this faith, thou
wilt prove a notable argument.   243

BENEDICK   If I do, hang me in a bottle like a cat and   244
shoot at me; and he that hits me, let him be clapped on
the shoulder and called Adam.   246

PEDRO   Well, as time shall try.
"In time the savage bull doth bear the yoke."   248

BENEDICK   The savage bull may, but if ever the sensible   249
Benedick bear it, pluck off the bull's horns and set   250
them in my forehead, and let me be vilely painted, and
in such great letters as they write "Here is good horse to
hire," let them signify under my sign "Here you may
see Benedick the married man."

CLAUDIO   If this should ever happen, thou wouldst be
horn-mad.   256

PEDRO   Nay, if Cupid have not spent all his quiver in
Venice, thou wilt quake for this shortly.   258

---

230 *hang . . . baldrick* hang my horn on an invisible shoulder belt (i.e., be
unaware of my cuckoldry)   **233** *fine* finis, conclusion   **234** *finer* more richly
dressed (because spared the expense of a wife)   **237–38** *lose . . . love* (lover's
sighs were supposed to consume blood)   **239** *pick out . . . pen* i.e., let me be
blinded by weeping over love laments   **240** *sign* printed sign hung outside a
shop, inn, or brothel   **243** *notable argument* famous example   **244** *bottle*
basket or cage (cats were shot as targets)   **246** *Adam* i.e., Adam Bell, a famous archer   **248** *"In time . . . yoke"* (proverbial)   **249** *sensible* sensitive
256 *horn-mad* raving mad, also mad with jealousy   **258** *Venice* (famous for
prostitutes); *quake* i.e., with fear (with pun on "quiver")

BENEDICK   I look for an earthquake too then.

260 PEDRO   Well, you will temporize with the hours. In the meantime, good Signor Benedick, repair to Leonato's, commend me to him and tell him I will not fail him at supper, for indeed he hath made great preparation.

264 BENEDICK   I have almost matter enough in me for such an embassage, and so I commit you –

266 CLAUDIO   To the tuition of God. From my house – if I had it –

PEDRO   The sixth of July. Your loving friend, Benedick.

BENEDICK   Nay, mock not, mock not. The body of your
270 discourse is sometime guarded with fragments, and the
271 guards are but slightly basted on neither. Ere you flout old ends any further, examine your conscience. And so I leave you.   *Exit.*

CLAUDIO
274 My liege, your highness now may do me good.

PEDRO
My love is thine to teach. Teach it but how,
276 And thou shalt see how apt it is to learn
Any hard lesson that may do thee good.

CLAUDIO
Hath Leonato any son, my lord?

PEDRO
No child but Hero; she's his only heir.
280 Dost thou affect her, Claudio?

CLAUDIO   O my lord,
281 When you went onward on this ended action,
I looked upon her with a soldier's eye,
That liked, but had a rougher task in hand
Than to drive liking to the name of love.

---

260 *temporize with the hours* weaken with time ("hours" may pun on "whores," pronounced similarly)   **264** *matter* sense   **266** *tuition* protection (Claudio is imitating the formal close of a letter)   **270** *guarded* trimmed   **271** *basted* lightly sewed   **271–72** *flout old ends* mock tag ends of wisdom (or cloth)   **274** *do me good* do me a favor   **276** *apt* ready   **280** *affect* love, aim at   **281** *ended action* war just ended

But now I am returned and that war thoughts   285
Have left their places vacant, in their rooms
Come thronging soft and delicate desires,
All prompting me how fair young Hero is,   288
Saying I liked her ere I went to wars.

PEDRO
Thou wilt be like a lover presently   290
And tire the hearer with a book of words.   291
If thou dost love fair Hero, cherish it,
And I will break with her and with her father,   293
And thou shalt have her. Was't not to this end
That thou began'st to twist so fine a story?   295

CLAUDIO
How sweetly you do minister to love,
That know love's grief by his complexion!   297
But lest my liking might too sudden seem,
I would have salved it with a longer treatise.   299

PEDRO
What need the bridge much broader than the flood?   300
The fairest grant is the necessity.   301
Look, what will serve is fit. 'Tis once, thou lovest,   302
And I will fit thee with the remedy.
I know we shall have reveling tonight.
I will assume thy part in some disguise
And tell fair Hero I am Claudio,
And in her bosom I'll unclasp my heart   307
And take her hearing prisoner with the force
And strong encounter of my amorous tale.
Then after to her father will I break,   310
And the conclusion is, she shall be thine.
In practice let us put it presently.   *Exeunt.*   312

*

---

285 *that* because   288 *prompting* reminding   291 *book of words* volume of
pretty speeches   293 *break with* broach the subject to   295 *twist* (cf. "spin a
yarn")   297 *complexion* appearance (referring to the lover's pallor)   299
salved smoothed over; *treatise* discourse   301 *The . . . necessity* the best gift is
whatever is needed   302 *once* once for all   307 *in her bosom* in private to her
312 *presently* immediately

∾ **I.2** *Enter Leonato and an old man [Antonio], brother
to Leonato [meeting].*

1 LEONATO   How now, brother? Where is my cousin your
   son? Hath he provided this music?
   ANTONIO   He is very busy about it. But, brother, I can
   tell you strange news that you yet dreamt not of.
   LEONATO   Are they good?
6 ANTONIO   As the event stamps them; but they have a
   good cover, they show well outward. The prince and
8 Count Claudio, walking in a thick-pleached alley in
9 mine orchard, were thus much overheard by a man of
10 mine: the prince discovered to Claudio that he loved
   my niece your daughter and meant to acknowledge it
12 this night in a dance, and, if he found her accordant, he
13 meant to take the present time by the top and instantly
   break with you of it.
   LEONATO   Hath the fellow any wit that told you this?
   ANTONIO   A good sharp fellow. I will send for him, and
   question him yourself.
   LEONATO   No, no. We will hold it as a dream till it
19 appear itself, but I will acquaint my daughter withal,
20 that she may be the better prepared for an answer, if
21 peradventure this be true. Go you and tell her of it.

I.2 The house of Leonato **s.d.** *old man* (editors assume that the unnamed old
brother of this scene, Leonato's brother Antonio [named at V.1.91], and the
Antonio of II.1.107 are all the same person, growing in identity as Shakespeare wrote the play) **1** *cousin* kinsman (this nephew is never referred to
again and by V.1.279 has ceased to exist; Shakespeare seems to have slimmed
down the household, for a cousin of Hero ought to have challenged Claudio
later in the play) **6** *event stamps* outcome determines (the figure is of a
printed newsbook) **8** *thick-pleached alley* walk lined by trees with interwoven branches **9** *orchard* garden (Shakespeare seems, perhaps carelessly, to
have imagined that the conversation at the end of I.1 was repeated in the orchard) **10** *discovered* disclosed **12** *accordant* agreeable **13** *take . . . top*
seize the moment **19** *appear* show **21** *peradventure* perhaps

[Enter various people.]

Cousins, you know what you have to do. – O, I cry you   22
mercy, friend. Go you with me, and I will use your
skill. – Good cousin, have a care this busy time.

Exeunt.

*

∾ **I.3** *Enter [Don] John the Bastard and Conrad, his
companion.*

CONRAD   What the goodyear, my lord! Why are you thus   1
out of measure sad?   2
JOHN   There is no measure in the occasion that breeds, 3
therefore the sadness is without limit.
CONRAD   You should hear reason.
JOHN   And when I have heard it, what blessing brings it?
CONRAD   If not a present remedy, at least a patient
sufferance.   8
JOHN   I wonder that thou (being, as thou sayst thou art,
born under Saturn) goest about to apply a moral medi-   10
cine to a mortifying mischief. I cannot hide what I am: 11
I must be sad when I have cause, and smile at no man's
jests; eat when I have stomach, and wait for no man's   13
leisure; sleep when I am drowsy, and tend on no
man's business; laugh when I am merry, and claw no   15
man in his humor.
CONRAD   Yea, but you must not make the full show of
this till you may do it without controlment. You have   18
of late stood out against your brother, and he hath ta'en 19

---

21 s.d. (some of Leonato's kinsmen, servants, and, perhaps, a musician or
two, whose "skill" [l. 24] Leonato will make use of, might be among those
bustling across the stage here)   **22–23** *cry you mercy* beg your pardon

I.3 1 *What the goodyear* (mild expostulation, "what the heck")   **2** *out of
measure* immoderately   **3** *breeds* causes it   **8** *sufferance* endurance   **10** *born
under Saturn* saturnine, ill-disposed; *moral* philosophical   **11** *mortifying mischief* deadly disease   **13** *stomach* appetite   **15** *claw* flatter   **18** *controlment*
restraint   **19** *stood out* rebelled

20   you newly into his grace, where it is impossible you
      should take true root but by the fair weather that you
22   make yourself. It is needful that you frame the season
      for your own harvest.

24 JOHN   I had rather be a canker in a hedge than a rose in
25   his grace, and it better fits my blood to be disdained of
26   all than to fashion a carriage to rob love from any. In
      this, though I cannot be said to be a flattering honest
      man, it must not be denied but I am a plain-dealing vil-
29   lain. I am trusted with a muzzle and enfranchised with
30   a clog, therefore I have decreed not to sing in my cage.
      If I had my mouth, I would bite; if I had my liberty, I
      would do my liking. In the meantime let me be that I
      am, and seek not to alter me.

   CONRAD   Can you make no use of your discontent?

   JOHN   I make all use of it, for I use it only. Who comes
36   here? *Enter Borachio.* What news, Borachio?

   BORACHIO   I came yonder from a great supper. The
      prince your brother is royally entertained by Leonato,
39   and I can give you intelligence of an intended marriage.

40 JOHN   Will it serve for any model to build mischief on?
41   What is he for a fool that betroths himself to unquiet-
      ness?

43 BORACHIO   Marry, it is your brother's right hand.

   JOHN   Who? the most exquisite Claudio?

   BORACHIO   Even he.

46 JOHN   A proper squire! And who? and who? which way
      looks he?

   BORACHIO   Marry, one Hero, the daughter and heir of
      Leonato.

---

20 *grace* favor   22 *frame* create   24 *canker* wild dog rose (despised as a
weed)   25 *blood* humor, temper   26 *fashion a carriage* assume a manner; *rob
love* gain love undeserved   29 *with a muzzle* but muzzled (i.e., not fully
trusted)   29–30 *enfranchised with a clog* freed, but with a ball and chain   36
Borachio (from Spanish for "wine bottle," hence "drunkard")   39 *intelligence*
news   41 *What is he for a fool* what fool is he   43 *Marry* why, to be sure
(originally an oath on the name of the Virgin Mary)   46 *proper squire* fine
fellow (contemptuous)

JOHN   A very forward March chick! How came you to ·50
this?

BORACHIO   Being entertained for a perfumer, as I was 52
smoking a musty room, comes me the prince and 53
Claudio, hand in hand in sad conference. I whipped me 54
behind the arras and there heard it agreed upon that 55
the prince should woo Hero for himself, and having
obtained her, give her to Count Claudio.

JOHN   Come, come, let us thither. This may prove food
to my displeasure. That young start-up hath all the
glory of my overthrow. If I can cross him any way, I 60
bless myself every way. You are both sure, and will assist 61
me?

CONRAD   To the death, my lord.

JOHN   Let us to the great supper. Their cheer is the
greater that I am subdued. Would the cook were o' my 65
mind! Shall we go prove what's to be done? 66

BORACHIO   We'll wait upon your lordship.   *[Exeunt.]*

✳

◆   **II.1**   *Enter Leonato, his brother [Antonio], Hero his*
daughter, and Beatrice his niece [, also Margaret and
Ursula].

LEONATO   Was not Count John here at supper?

ANTONIO   I saw him not.

BEATRICE   How tartly that gentleman looks! I never can 3
see him but I am heartburned an hour after. 4

HERO   He is of a very melancholy disposition.

---

50 *forward March chick* precocious youngster   52 *entertained for* hired as
53 *smoking* sweetening the smell with the smoke of burning herbs   54 *sad*
serious (this is yet another account of the conversation at the end of I.1,
which was, supposedly, repeated in the orchard, according to I.2.9–10)   55
arras tapestry wall hanging   61 *sure* trustworthy   65–66 *o' my mind* i.e.,
disposed to poison them   66 *prove* try

    II.1 s.d. (Q adds Leonato's wife [see n. to I.1 s.d.] and an unnamed, mute
kinsman; Q gives no entry in the scene for Margaret and Ursula, who are
more likely to enter with the rest of Leonato's household than with the
maskers)   3 *tartly* sour   4 *am heartburned* have indigestion

6   BEATRICE   He were an excellent man that were made just
in the midway between him and Benedick. The one is
8   too like an image and says nothing, and the other too
9   like my lady's eldest son, evermore tattling.

10   LEONATO   Then half Signor Benedick's tongue in Count
John's mouth, and half Count John's melancholy in
Signor Benedick's face –

13   BEATRICE   With a good leg and a good foot, uncle, and
14   money enough in his purse, such a man would win any
15   woman in the world – if a could get her good will.

    LEONATO   By my troth, niece, thou wilt never get thee a
17   husband if thou be so shrewd of thy tongue.

18   ANTONIO   In faith, she's too curst.

19   BEATRICE   Too curst is more than curst. I shall lessen
20   God's sending that way, for it is said, "God sends a
21   curst cow short horns," but to a cow too curst he sends
none.

    LEONATO   So, by being too curst, God will send you no
horns.

25   BEATRICE   Just, if he send me no husband, for the which
blessing I am at him upon my knees every morning and
evening. Lord, I could not endure a husband with a
28   beard on his face. I had rather lie in the woolen!

29   LEONATO   You may light on a husband that hath no
30   beard.

    BEATRICE   What should I do with him? dress him in my
apparel and make him my waiting gentlewoman? He
that hath a beard is more than a youth, and he that
hath no beard is less than a man; and he that is more
than a youth is not for me, and he that is less than a

---

6 *He were* that man would be   8 *image* statue   9 *my lady's eldest son* a spoiled
child who talks too much   13 *foot* (often a euphemism for "penis")   14
purse (punning on "scrotum")   15 *good will* (1) agreement, (2) sexual desire,
(3) genitalia   17 *shrewd* satirical   18 *curst* shrewish, ill-tempered   19 *Too*
(punning on "two")   20 *that way* in that respect   21 *short horns* (punning
on "small penises")   25 *Just* exactly; *no husband* (because she will not have
sex and hence will not cuckold him)   28 *in the woolen* between blankets
without sheets   29 *light on* find

man, I am not for him. Therefore I will even take sixpence in earnest of the bearherd and lead his apes into   37
hell.

LEONATO   Well then, go you into hell?

BEATRICE   No, but to the gate, and there will the devil   40
meet me like an old cuckold with horns on his head,
and say, "Get you to heaven, Beatrice, get you to
heaven. Here's no place for you maids." So deliver I up
my apes, and away to Saint Peter. For the heavens, he   44
shows me where the bachelors sit, and there live we as   45
merry as the day is long.

ANTONIO   [To Hero] Well, niece, I trust you will be ruled
by your father.

BEATRICE   Yes, faith. It is my cousin's duty to make   49
curtsy and say, "Father, as it please you." But yet for all   50
that, cousin, let him be a handsome fellow, or else make
another curtsy, and say, "Father, as it please me."

LEONATO   Well, niece, I hope to see you one day fitted
with a husband.

BEATRICE   Not till God make men of some other metal   55
than earth. Would it not grieve a woman to be over-
mastered with a piece of valiant dust? to make an account of her life to a clod of wayward marl? No, uncle,   58
I'll none. Adam's sons are my brethren, and truly I hold
it a sin to match in my kindred.   60

LEONATO   [To Hero] Daughter, remember what I told
you. If the prince do solicit you in that kind, you know   62
your answer.

BEATRICE   The fault will be in the music, cousin, if you
be not wooed in good time. If the prince be too impor-   65
tant, tell him there is measure in everything, and so   66

---

37 *in earnest* as deposit; *bearherd* (who often also kept trained apes); *lead his
apes* (the proverbial punishment of women who die virgins)   44 *For the
heavens* i.e., (1) as my share of heavens, (2) in front of ("'fore"), (3) as an exclamation   45 *bachelors* unmarried men and women   49–50 *make curtsy*
curtsy, show respect   55 *metal* material   58 *marl* clay, earth   60 *match . . .
kindred* i.e., wed a brother   62 *solicit . . . kind* propose   65–66 *important*
importunate   66 *measure* moderation (but also a stately dance)

dance out the answer. For, hear me, Hero: wooing,
wedding, and repenting is as a Scotch jig, a measure,
69 and a cinquepace. The first suit is hot and hasty like a
70 Scotch jig (and full as fantastical); the wedding, man-
71 nerly modest, as a measure, full of state and ancientry;
and then comes Repentance and with his bad legs falls
into the cinquepace faster and faster, till he sink into
his grave.
75 LEONATO   Cousin, you apprehend passing shrewdly.
BEATRICE   I have a good eye, uncle, I can see a church by
daylight.
LEONATO   The revelers are entering, brother. Make good
79 room.
  Enter [masked] Prince [Don] Pedro, Claudio, and
  Benedick, and Balthasar; [also, unmasked,] Don John
  [and Borachio and Musicians, including a Drummer.
  The dance begins].
80 PEDRO   *[To Hero]* Lady, will you walk a bout with your
81 friend?
HERO   So you walk softly and look sweetly and say nothing, I am yours for the walk; and especially when I walk
away.
PEDRO   With me in your company?
HERO   I may say so when I please.
PEDRO   And when please you to say so?
88 HERO   When I like your favor, for God defend the lute
should be like the case!
90 PEDRO   My visor is Philemon's roof; within the house is
Jove.

---

69 *cinquepace* lively dance (pronounced "sink-a-pace," hence the pun at l.
73); *suit* courtship   **71** *state* dignity; *ancientry* traditional formality   **75** *apprehend passing shrewdly* perceive with unusual sharpness   **79 s.d.** (F adds
"Maskers with a drum" to Q's s.d.; at some point after l. 79 Antonio needs to
put on a mask)   **80** *a bout* a turn   **81** *friend* a lover of either sex   **88** *favor*
face; *defend* forbid, prevent   **88–89** *lute . . . case* i.e., your face should be like
your mask   **90–93** (a rhyming couplet in fourteeners)   **90** *visor* mask;
Philemon an old peasant who entertained Jove and Mercury in his humble
cottage

HERO   Why then, your visor should be thatched.   92

PEDRO   Speak low if you speak love.

   [They dance aside.]

BALTHASAR   *[To Margaret]* Well, I would you did like me.

MARGARET   So would not I for your own sake, for I have
many ill qualities.   96

BALTHASAR   Which is one?

MARGARET   I say my prayers aloud.

BALTHASAR   I love you the better. The hearers may cry
amen.   100

MARGARET   God match me with a good dancer!

BALTHASAR   Amen.

MARGARET   And God keep him out of my sight when
the dance is done! Answer, clerk.   104

BALTHASAR   No more words. The clerk is answered.

   [They dance aside.]

URSULA   *[To Antonio]* I know you well enough. You are
Signor Antonio.

ANTONIO   At a word, I am not.

URSULA   I know you by the waggling of your head.   109

ANTONIO   To tell you true, I counterfeit him.   110

URSULA   You could never do him so ill-well unless you   111
were the very man. Here's his dry hand up and down.   112
You are he, you are he!

ANTONIO   At a word, I am not.

URSULA   Come, come, do you think I do not know you
by your excellent wit? Can virtue hide itself? Go to,
mum, you are he. Graces will appear, and there's an end.   117

   [They dance aside.]

BEATRICE   *[To Benedick]* Will you not tell me who told
you so?

BENEDICK   No, you shall pardon me.   120

BEATRICE   Nor will you not tell me who you are?

---

92 *thatched* i.e., whiskered **96** *qualities* traits of character **104** *clerk* (the
parish clerk read the responses in church services) **109** *waggling* shaking
(with old age?) **111** *do him so ill-well* imitate his ills so well **112** *dry hand*
(a sign of age); *up and down* exactly **117** *Graces* good qualities

BENEDICK   Not now.

BEATRICE   That I was disdainful, and that I had my good
124   wit out of the *Hundred Merry Tales*. Well, this was
Signor Benedick that said so.

BENEDICK   What's he?

BEATRICE   I am sure you know him well enough.

BENEDICK   Not I, believe me.

BEATRICE   Did he never make you laugh?

130   BENEDICK   I pray you, what is he?

BEATRICE   Why, he is the prince's jester, a very dull fool.
132   Only his gift is in devising impossible slanders. None
133   but libertines delight in him, and the commendation is
134   not in his wit, but in his villainy, for he both pleases
men and angers them, and then they laugh at him and
136   beat him. I am sure he is in the fleet. I would he had
137   boarded me.

BENEDICK   When I know the gentleman, I'll tell him
what you say.

140   BEATRICE   Do, do. He'll but break a comparison or two
on me; which peradventure, not marked or not laughed
at, strikes him into melancholy, and then there's a
143   partridge wing saved, for the fool will eat no supper
144   that night. *[Music.]* We must follow the leaders.

BENEDICK   In every good thing.

BEATRICE   Nay, if they lead to any ill, I will leave them at
the next turning.

Dance. Exeunt [all but Don John,
Borachio, and Claudio].

JOHN   *[To Borachio]* Sure my brother is amorous on Hero
and hath withdrawn her father to break with him about
150   it. The ladies follow her and but one visor remains.

---

124 *Hundred Merry Tales* a popular book of crude comic stories, first published in 1526   132 *Only his gift* his only gift; *impossible* incredible   133
libertines freethinkers, loose livers   134 *villainy* rudeness   136 *fleet* company of maskers (with play on "sea fleet")   137 *boarded* assaulted (nautical
term)   140 *break a comparison* tilt with words   143 *partridge wing* (considered a great delicacy)   144 *leaders* (in the dance)

BORACHIO　And that is Claudio. I know him by his
bearing.

JOHN　*[To Claudio]* Are not you Signor Benedick?

CLAUDIO　You know me well. I am he.

JOHN　Signor, you are very near my brother in his love.
He is enamored on Hero. I pray you dissuade him from
her; she is no equal for his birth. You may do the part of
an honest man in it.

CLAUDIO　How know you he loves her?

JOHN　I heard him swear his affection.　　　　　　160

BORACHIO　So did I too, and he swore he would marry
her tonight.

JOHN　Come, let us to the banquet.　　　　　　163

Exeunt. Manet Claudio.

CLAUDIO

Thus answer I in name of Benedick

But hear these ill news with the ears of Claudio.

'Tis certain so. The prince woos for himself.

Friendship is constant in all other things

Save in the office and affairs of love.　　　　168

Therefore all hearts in love use their own tongues.　169

Let every eye negotiate for itself　　　　　　*170*

And trust no agent, for beauty is a witch

Against whose charms faith melteth into blood.　172

This is an accident of hourly proof,　　　　　173

Which I mistrusted not. Farewell therefore Hero!　174

Enter Benedick.

BENEDICK　Count Claudio?

CLAUDIO　Yea, the same.

BENEDICK　Come, will you go with me?

CLAUDIO　Whither?

BENEDICK　Even to the next willow, about your own
business, county. What fashion will you wear the　180

---

163 *banquet* light dessert after "supper," II.1.1　168 *office* business, employment　169 *all* let all　172 *blood* passion　173 *accident . . . proof* common
occurrence　174 *mistrusted* suspected　180 *county* count

181   garland of? about your neck, like an usurer's chain? or
182   under your arm, like a lieutenant's scarf? You must wear
     it one way, for the prince hath got your Hero.

    CLAUDIO   I wish him joy of her.

185 BENEDICK Why, that's spoken like an honest drover. So
     they sell bullocks. But did you think the prince would
     have served you thus?

    CLAUDIO   I pray you leave me.

189 BENEDICK Ho! now you strike like the blind man! 'Twas
190   the boy that stole your meat, and you'll beat the post.

191 CLAUDIO   If it will not be, I'll leave you.   *Exit.*

    BENEDICK   Alas, poor hurt fowl, now will he creep into
193   sedges. But, that my Lady Beatrice should know me,
     and not know me! The prince's fool! Ha! it may be I go
     under that title because I am merry. Yea, but so I am
     apt to do myself wrong. I am not so reputed. It is the
197   base (though bitter) disposition of Beatrice that puts
198   the world into her person and so gives me out. Well, I'll
199   be revenged as I may.

    Enter the Prince [Don Pedro].

200 PEDRO   Now, signor, where's the count? Did you see
     him?

202 BENEDICK   Troth, my lord, I have played the part of Lady
203   Fame. I found him here as melancholy as a lodge in a
     warren. I told him, and I think I told him true, that
     your grace had got the good will of this young lady, and

---

181 *garland* i.e., of willow, symbol of forsaken love; *about your neck* i.e., as a symbol of wealth   182 *under your arm* across your chest   185 *drover* cattle trader   189 *the blind man* (unidentified allusion to a proverb or familiar story)   190 *post* (1) pillar, (2) messenger   191 *If . . . be* if you will not go   193 *sedges* reeds   197 *bitter* biting   197–98 *puts . . . person* attributes to the world her own personal feelings   198 *gives me out* reports me   199 **s.d.** (Q's s.d. here is almost certainly wrong in giving entrances for Don John, Borachio, and Conrad; F gives an entry for Don Pedro alone, but Hero and Leonato could enter here [as in Q] and stand apart, rather than entering at, say, 247 with Claudio and Beatrice, where F marks their entry – this would make Benedick's "this young lady," at l. 205, a direct reference – or they could enter at l. 284)   202–3 *Lady Fame* bearer of tidings   203–4 *lodge . . . warren* gamekeeper's hut in a game reserve (symbol of isolation)

I offered him my company to a willow tree, either to
make him a garland, as being forsaken, or to bind him
up a rod, as being worthy to be whipped.

PEDRO   To be whipped? What's his fault?

BENEDICK   The flat transgression of a schoolboy who,   210
being overjoyed with finding a bird's nest, shows it his
companion, and he steals it.

PEDRO   Wilt thou make a trust a transgression? The
transgression is in the stealer.

BENEDICK   Yet it had not been amiss the rod had been
made, and the garland too, for the garland he might
have worn himself, and the rod he might have bestowed on you, who, as I take it, have stolen his bird's
nest.

PEDRO   I will but teach them to sing and restore them to   220
the owner.

BENEDICK   If their singing answer your saying, by my   222
faith you say honestly.

PEDRO   The Lady Beatrice hath a quarrel to you. The
gentleman that danced with her told her she is much
wronged by you.   226

BENEDICK   O, she misused me past the endurance of a   227
block! An oak but with one green leaf on it would have
answered her; my very visor began to assume life and
scold with her. She told me, not thinking I had been   230
myself, that I was the prince's jester, that I was duller
than a great thaw, huddling jest upon jest with such   232
impossible conveyance upon me that I stood like a man   233
at a mark, with a whole army shooting at me. She   234
speaks poniards, and every word stabs. If her breath   235
were as terrible as her terminations, there were no liv-   236
ing near her; she would infect to the North Star. I   237

---

210 *flat* plain   222 *If . . . saying* if it turns out as you say   226 *wronged* slandered   227 *misused* abused   232 *thaw* (when roads are impassable and one
must stay at home)   233 *impossible conveyance* incredible dexterity   234 *at
a mark* beside a target   235 *poniards* daggers   236 *terminations* terms (i.e.,
name-calling)   237 *infect* emit foul odors (supposed to carry infection)

would not marry her though she were endowed with all
that Adam had left him before he transgressed. She
240 would have made Hercules have turned spit, yea, and
have cleft his club to make the fire too. Come, talk not
242 of her. You shall find her the infernal Ate in good ap-
243 parel. I would to God some scholar would conjure her,
for certainly, while she is here, a man may live as quiet
in hell as in a sanctuary, and people sin upon purpose,
because they would go thither. So indeed all disquiet,
247 horror, and perturbation follows her.

    Enter Claudio and Beatrice [, Leonato and Hero].

PEDRO Look, here she comes.

BENEDICK Will your grace command me any service to
250 the world's end? I will go on the slightest errand now to
the Antipodes that you can devise to send me on, I will
252 fetch you a toothpicker now from the furthest inch of
253 Asia, bring you the length of Prester John's foot, fetch
254 you a hair off the Great Cham's beard, do you any em-
255 bassage to the Pygmies, rather than hold three words'
256 conference with this harpy. You have no employment
for me?

PEDRO None, but to desire your good company.

BENEDICK O God, sir, here's a dish I love not! I cannot
260 endure my Lady Tongue.   *Exit.*

PEDRO Come, lady, come, you have lost the heart of
Signor Benedick.

BEATRICE Indeed, my lord, he lent it me awhile, and I
264 gave him use for it – a double heart for his single one.

---

240 *Hercules . . . spit* (The Amazon Omphale enslaved Hercules and set him
to spinning dressed as a woman. Turning a spit was an even more humble
chore, assigned to a boy or even a dog.) 242 *Ate* goddess of discord 243
conjure her (scholars were supposed to have the power to call up or dismiss
evil spirits) 247 *follows* attends on 252 *toothpicker* toothpick 253 *Prester
John* a mythical Christian monarch of Ethiopia 254 *Cham* Khan of Tartary,
ruler of the Mongols 255 *Pygmies* a legendary race of dwarfs said to dwell
in Ethiopia or in the Far East 256 *harpy* a mythical predatory creature, with
a woman's face and body and a bird's wings and claws 264 *use* interest
264–65 *double heart . . . dice* (she gave him her heart but he deceived her)

Marry, once before he won it of me with false dice;
therefore your grace may well say I have lost it.

PEDRO   You have put him down, lady; you have put him   267
down.

BEATRICE   So I would not he should do me, my lord, lest
I should prove the mother of fools. I have brought   270
Count Claudio, whom you sent me to seek.

PEDRO   Why, how now, count? Wherefore are you sad?

CLAUDIO   Not sad, my lord.

PEDRO   How then? Sick?

CLAUDIO   Neither, my lord.

BEATRICE   The count is neither sad, nor sick, nor merry,
nor well; but civil count – civil as an orange, and some-   277
thing of that jealous complexion.   278

PEDRO   I' faith, lady, I think your blazon to be true,   279
though I'll be sworn, if he be so, his conceit is false.   280
Here, Claudio, I have wooed in thy name, and fair
Hero is won. I have broke with her father, and his good
will obtained. Name the day of marriage, and God give
thee joy!

LEONATO   Count, take of me my daughter, and with her
my fortunes. His grace hath made the match, and all   286
grace say amen to it!

BEATRICE   Speak, count, 'tis your cue.

CLAUDIO   Silence is the perfectest herald of joy. I were
but little happy if I could say how much. *[To Hero]*   290
Lady, as you are mine, I am yours. I give away myself
for you and dote upon the exchange.

BEATRICE   *[To Hero]* Speak, cousin, or, if you cannot, stop
his mouth with a kiss and let not him speak neither.

267–68 *put him down* humiliated him (Beatrice at 269 punningly takes it as
"having sex with him")   **277** *civil* grave, sober (with a pun on "oranges of
Seville")   **278** *of . . . complexion* i.e., yellow (symbolic of jealousy)   **279** *blazon* description (heraldic term)   **280** *conceit* conception, idea (with the addi-
tional suggestion here, after *blazon*, of the fanciful device painted on a
knight's shield)   **286–87** *all grace* i.e., God, the source of all grace

PEDRO   In faith, lady, you have a merry heart.

296 BEATRICE   Yea, my lord, I thank it. Poor fool, it keeps on
297   the windy side of care. My cousin tells him in his ear
      that he is in her heart.

CLAUDIO   And so she doth, cousin.

300 BEATRICE   Good Lord, for alliance! Thus goes everyone
301   to the world but I, and I am sunburned. I may sit in a
302   corner and cry "Heigh-ho for a husband!"

303 PEDRO   Lady Beatrice, I will get you one.

BEATRICE   I would rather have one of your father's
305   getting. Hath your grace ne'er a brother like you? Your
      father got excellent husbands, if a maid could come by
      them.

PEDRO   Will you have me, lady?

BEATRICE   No, my lord, unless I might have another for
310   working days: your grace is too costly to wear every day.
      But I beseech your grace pardon me. I was born to
312   speak all mirth and no matter.

PEDRO   Your silence most offends me, and to be merry
      best becomes you, for out o' question you were born in
      a merry hour.

BEATRICE   No, sure, my lord, my mother cried, but then
      there was a star danced, and under that was I born. [To
      Hero and Claudio] Cousins, God give you joy!

319 LEONATO   Niece, will you look to those things I told you
320   of?

321 BEATRICE   I cry you mercy, uncle. [To Don Pedro] By
      your grace's pardon.   Exit Beatrice.

PEDRO   By my troth, a pleasant-spirited lady.

LEONATO   There's little of the melancholy element in
      her, my lord. She is never sad but when she sleeps, and

---

296 *fool* innocent creature   297 *windy* windward, safe   300 *for alliance*
(Claudio has just called her *cousin* in anticipation of becoming her cousin by
marriage)   300–01 *goes . . . world* everybody gets married   301 *sunburned*
i.e., suntanned and therefore unattractive   302 *"Heigh-ho for a husband"*
(from an old song)   303 *get* procure   305 *getting* begetting   312 *matter*
substance   319–20 (Does Leonato invent those tasks to cover an awkward
moment?)   321–22 *By your grace's pardon* excuse me

not ever sad then, for I have heard my daughter say she
hath often dreamt of unhappiness and waked herself
with laughing.

PEDRO   She cannot endure to hear tell of a husband.

LEONATO   O, by no means! She mocks all her wooers out   330
of suit.

PEDRO   She were an excellent wife for Benedick.

LEONATO   O Lord, my lord, if they were but a week married, they would talk themselves mad.

PEDRO   County Claudio, when mean you to go to
church?

CLAUDIO   Tomorrow, my lord. Time goes on crutches till
Love have all his rites.

LEONATO   Not till Monday, my dear son, which is hence
a just sevennight, and a time too brief too, to have all   340
things answer my mind.   341

PEDRO   Come, you shake the head at so long a breathing,
but I warrant thee, Claudio, the time shall not go dully
by us. I will in the interim undertake one of Hercules'
labors, which is, to bring Signor Benedick and the Lady
Beatrice into a mountain of affection th' one with th'
other. I would fain have it a match, and I doubt not but   347
to fashion it if you three will but minister such assistance as I shall give you direction.

LEONATO   My lord, I am for you, though it cost me ten   350
nights' watchings.   351

CLAUDIO   And I, my lord.

PEDRO   And you too, gentle Hero?

HERO   I will do any modest office, my lord, to help my
cousin to a good husband.

PEDRO   And Benedick is not the unhopefulest husband
that I know. Thus far can I praise him: he is of a noble
strain, of approved valor, and confirmed honesty. I will   358
teach you how to humor your cousin, that she shall fall

330–31 *mocks . . . suit* makes fun of them until they do not dare to woo her
341 *answer my mind* as I wish them   347 *fain* gladly   351 *watchings* staying
awake   358 *strain* family

360 in love with Benedick; and I, *[To Leonato and Claudio]*
361 with your two helps, will so practice on Benedick that, in
362 despite of his quick wit and his queasy stomach, he shall
fall in love with Beatrice. If we can do this, Cupid is no
longer an archer; his glory shall be ours, for we are the
only love gods. Go in with me, and I will tell you my
366 drift.   *Exit [with the others].*

*

～ **II.2** *Enter [Don] John and Borachio.*

JOHN It is so. The Count Claudio shall marry the
daughter of Leonato.

BORACHIO Yea, my lord, but I can cross it.

JOHN Any bar, any cross, any impediment will be
5   medicinable to me. I am sick in displeasure to him, and
6   whatsoever comes athwart his affection ranges evenly
with mine. How canst thou cross this marriage?

8 BORACHIO Not honestly, my lord, but so covertly that
no dishonesty shall appear in me.

10 JOHN Show me briefly how.

BORACHIO I think I told your lordship, a year since, how
much I am in the favor of Margaret, the waiting gentlewoman to Hero.

JOHN I remember.

BORACHIO I can, at any unseasonable instant of the
night, appoint her to look out at her lady's chamber
window.

JOHN What life is in that to be the death of this marriage?

20 BORACHIO The poison of that lies in you to temper. Go
you to the prince your brother, spare not to tell him
that he hath wronged his honor in marrying the

361–62 *in despite* in spite   362 *queasy* delicate   366 *drift* plan
   II.2   5 *medicinable* curative   6–7 *whatsoever . . . mine* whatever vexes his
love suits me   8 *covertly* secretly   20 *temper* compound, mix

renowned Claudio (whose estimation do you mightily 23
hold up) to a contaminated stale, such a one as Hero.   24
JOHN What proof shall I make of that?
BORACHIO Proof enough to misuse the prince, to vex
Claudio, to undo Hero, and kill Leonato. Look you for
any other issue?
JOHN Only to despite them I will endeavor anything.   29
BORACHIO Go then, find me a meet hour to draw Don 30
Pedro and the Count Claudio alone, tell them that you
know that Hero loves me, intend a kind of zeal both to 32
the prince and Claudio, as, in love of your brother's
honor, who hath made this match, and his friend's reputation, who is thus like to be cozened with the sem- 35
blance of a maid, that you have discovered thus. They
will scarcely believe this without trial. Offer them
instances, which shall bear no less likelihood than to 38
see me at her chamber window, hear me call Margaret
Hero, hear Margaret term me Claudio; and bring them 40
to see this the very night before the intended wedding
(for in the meantime I will so fashion the matter that
Hero shall be absent) and there shall appear such seeming truth of Hero's disloyalty that jealousy shall be 44
called assurance and all the preparation overthrown.   45
JOHN Grow this to what adverse issue it can, I will put it
in practice. Be cunning in the working this, and thy fee
is a thousand ducats.   48
BORACHIO Be you constant in the accusation, and my
cunning shall not shame me.   50
JOHN I will presently go learn their day of marriage.   51
                          Exit [with Borachio].

                          ✳

---

23 *estimation* reputation **24** *stale* prostitute **29** *despite* spite **30** *meet hour*
suitable time **32** *intend* pretend **35** *cozened* deceived, cheated **35–36**
semblance outward appearance **38** *instances* proofs **44** *jealousy* suspicion
45 *assurance* proof **48** *ducats* gold coins **51** *presently* immediately

∾ **II.3** *Enter Benedick alone.*

BENEDICK   Boy!
   [Enter Boy.]
BOY   Signor?
BENEDICK   In my chamber window lies a book. Bring it
hither to me in the orchard.
BOY   I am here already, sir.
BENEDICK   I know that, but I would have thee hence and
here again. *Exit [Boy].* I do much wonder that one
man, seeing how much another man is a fool when he
dedicates his behaviors to love, will, after he hath
10   laughed at such shallow follies in others, become the argument of his own scorn by falling in love; and such a
man is Claudio. I have known when there was no music
13   with him but the drum and the fife, and now had he
rather hear the tabor and the pipe. I have known when he
15   would have walked ten mile afoot to see a good armor,
16   and now will he lie ten nights awake carving the fashion
17   of a new doublet. He was wont to speak plain and to the
purpose, like an honest man and a soldier, and now is
19   he turned orthography; his words are a very fantastical
20   banquet – just so many strange dishes. May I be so
21   converted and see with these eyes? I cannot tell. I think
not. I will not be sworn but love may transform me to
an oyster; but I'll take my oath on it, till he have made
an oyster of me he shall never make me such a fool.
One woman is fair, yet I am well; another is wise, yet I
am well; another virtuous, yet I am well. But till all

II.3 **10–11** *argument* subject   **13–14** *drum . . . pipe* (drum and fife were
used for military music, tabor and pipe for festivities)   **15** *armor* suit of
armor   **16** *carving* designing   **17** *doublet* jacket   **19** *orthography* fashionable
and overelaborate in his choice and pronunciation of words   **21** *converted*
changed; *these eyes* the eyes of a lover

graces be in one woman, one woman shall not come in
my grace. Rich she shall be, that's certain; wise, or I'll
none; virtuous, or I'll never cheapen her; fair, or I'll   29
never look on her; mild, or come not near me; noble,   30
or not I for an angel; of good discourse, an excellent
musician, and her hair shall be of what color it please
God. Ha, the prince and Monsieur Love! I will hide me
in the arbor. *[He hides.]*
        Enter Prince [Don Pedro], Leonato, Claudio.

PEDRO
  Come, shall we hear this music?

CLAUDIO
  Yea, my good lord. How still the evening is,
  As hushed on purpose to grace harmony!

PEDRO
  See you where Benedick hath hid himself?

CLAUDIO
  O, very well, my lord. The music ended,
  We'll fit the kid fox with a pennyworth.   40
        Enter Balthasar with music.

PEDRO
  Come, Balthasar, we'll hear that song again.

BALTHASAR
  O, good my lord, tax not so bad a voice
  To slander music any more than once.

PEDRO
  It is the witness still of excellency   44
  To put a strange face on his own perfection.   45
  I pray thee sing, and let me woo no more.

BALTHASAR
  Because you talk of wooing, I will sing,

---

29 *cheapen* bargain for   **30–31** *noble . . . angel* (play on the names of gold
coins; the noble was worth about a third less than the angel)   **40** *fit . . . pennyworth* give the sly young fellow all he bargained for ("kid fox" is often
emended to "hid fox," a children's hiding game); **s.d.** *with music* (either
"with musicians" or "with a musical instrument")   **44** *witness* evidence   **45**
put . . . on pretend not to know

Since many a wooer doth commence his suit
To her he thinks not worthy, yet he woos,
50   Yet will he swear he loves.

PEDRO   Nay, pray thee come,
51   Or if thou wilt hold longer argument,
Do it in notes.

BALTHASAR   Note this before my notes:
There's not a note of mine that's worth the noting.

PEDRO
54   Why, these are very crotchets that he speaks!
55   Note notes, forsooth, and nothing!
     [Music.]

BENEDICK   *[Aside]* Now divine air! Now is his soul rav-
57   ished! Is it not strange that sheep's guts should hale
58   souls out of men's bodies? Well, a horn for my money,
when all's done.

BALTHASAR

The Song.
60   Sigh no more, ladies, sigh no more.
            Men were deceivers ever,
         One foot in sea, and one on shore,
            To one thing constant never.
               Then sigh not so,
               But let them go,
66   And be you blithe and bonny,
         Converting all your sounds of woe
         Into Hey nonny, nonny.

         Sing no more ditties, sing no moe,
70   Of dumps so dull and heavy.
         The fraud of men was ever so,
            Since summer first was leafy.
            Then sigh not so, etc.

---

51 *argument* talk   54 *crotchets* notes of half the value of a minim, quibbles
55 *nothing* (pronounced the same as *noting* above, and so punned on)   57
hale draw   58 *horn* (for hunting or military calls)   66 *bonny* carefree   70
dumps sad songs, usually love songs

PEDRO   By my troth, a good song.

BALTHASAR   And an ill singer, my lord.

PEDRO   Ha, no, no, faith! Thou sing'st well enough for a 76
shift.

BENEDICK   *[Aside]* An he had been a dog that should
have howled thus, they would have hanged him, and I
pray God his bad voice bode no mischief. I had as lief 80
have heard the night raven, come what plague could 81
have come after it.

PEDRO   Yea, marry. Dost thou hear, Balthasar? I pray
thee get us some excellent music, for tomorrow night
we would have it at the Lady Hero's chamber window.

BALTHASAR   The best I can, my lord.

PEDRO   Do so. Farewell. *Exit Balthasar [with music].*
Come hither, Leonato. What was it you told me of
today? that your niece Beatrice was in love with Signor
Benedick?   90

CLAUDIO   O, ay! – *[Aside to Pedro]* Stalk on, stalk on; the 91
fowl sits. – I did never think that lady would have loved
any man.

LEONATO   No, nor I neither, but most wonderful that
she should so dote on Signor Benedick, whom she hath
in all outward behaviors seemed ever to abhor.

BENEDICK   *[Aside]* Is't possible? Sits the wind in that
corner?

LEONATO   By my troth, my lord, I cannot tell what to
think of it, but that she loves him with an enragèd af- 100
fection, it is past the infinite of thought.   101

PEDRO   May be she doth but counterfeit.

CLAUDIO   Faith, like enough.

LEONATO   O God, counterfeit? There was never counterfeit of passion came so near the life of passion as she
discovers it.   106

PEDRO   Why, what effects of passion shows she?

76–77 *for a shift* at a pinch   80 *lief* willingly   81 *night raven* (portent of dis-
aster)   91–92 *the fowl sits* (the victim's ready)   100 *enragèd* frenzied   101
infinite furthest reach   106 *discovers* reveals

CLAUDIO   *[Aside]* Bait the hook well! This fish will bite.

LEONATO   What effects, my lord? She will sit you – you
110   heard my daughter tell you how.

CLAUDIO   She did indeed.

PEDRO   How, how, I pray you? You amaze me. I would
have thought her spirit had been invincible against all
assaults of affection.

LEONATO   I would have sworn it had, my lord – especially against Benedick.

117 BENEDICK   *[Aside]* I should think this a gull but that the
white-bearded fellow speaks it. Knavery cannot, sure,
hide himself in such reverence.

120 CLAUDIO   *[Aside]* He hath ta'en th' infection. Hold it up.

PEDRO   Hath she made her affection known to Benedick?

LEONATO   No, and swears she never will. That's her torment.

CLAUDIO   'Tis true indeed. So your daughter says. "Shall
I," says she, "that have so oft encountered him with
scorn, write to him that I love him?"

LEONATO   This says she now when she is beginning to
write to him, for she'll be up twenty times a night, and
129   there will she sit in her smock till she have writ a sheet
130   of paper. My daughter tells us all.

CLAUDIO   Now you talk of a sheet of paper, I remember
a pretty jest your daughter told us of.

LEONATO   O, when she had writ it, and was reading it
134   over, she found "Benedick" and "Beatrice" between the
sheet?

CLAUDIO   That.

LEONATO   O, she tore the letter into a thousand
138   halfpence, railed at herself that she should be so im-
139   modest to write to one that she knew would flout her.
140   "I measure him," says she, "by my own spirit, for I

---

117 *gull* hoax, trick   120 *Hold* keep   129 *smock* garment that served as both
slip and nightdress   134–35 *between the sheet* in the folded sheet of paper,
with pun on "bedsheets"   138 *halfpence* i.e., small pieces   139 *flout* mock

should flout him if he writ to me. Yea, though I love him, I should."

CLAUDIO   Then down upon her knees she falls, weeps, sobs, beats her heart, tears her hair, prays, curses – "O sweet Benedick! God give me patience!"

LEONATO   She doth indeed; my daughter says so. And the ecstasy hath so much overborne her that my daugh- 147 ter is sometime afeard she will do a desperate outrage to herself. It is very true.

PEDRO   It were good that Benedick knew of it by some 150 other, if she will not discover it.

CLAUDIO   To what end? He would make but a sport of it and torment the poor lady worse.

PEDRO   An he should, it were an alms to hang him! She's 154 an excellent sweet lady, and (out of all suspicion) she is virtuous.

CLAUDIO   And she is exceeding wise.

PEDRO   In everything but in loving Benedick.

LEONATO   O, my lord, wisdom and blood combating in 159 so tender a body, we have ten proofs to one that blood 160 hath the victory. I am sorry for her, as I have just cause, being her uncle and her guardian.

PEDRO   I would she had bestowed this dotage on me. I 163 would have doffed all other respects and made her half 164 myself. I pray you tell Benedick of it and hear what a will say.

LEONATO   Were it good, think you?

CLAUDIO   Hero thinks surely she will die, for she says she will die if he love her not, and she will die ere she make her love known, and she will die, if he woo her, rather 170 than she will bate one breath of her accustomed cross- 171 ness.

---

147 *ecstasy* excess of passion   154 *an alms* a good deed   159 *blood* nature, natural feeling, passion   163 *dotage* doting affection   164 *doffed* put aside; *respects* considerations   171 *bate* abate, give up

173 PEDRO   She doth well. If she should make tender of her
love, 'tis very possible he'll scorn it, for the man (as you
175   know all) hath a contemptible spirit.
176 CLAUDIO   He is a very proper man.
177 PEDRO   He hath indeed a good outward happiness.
CLAUDIO   Before God, and in my mind, very wise.
PEDRO   He doth indeed show some sparks that are like
180   wit.
CLAUDIO   And I take him to be valiant.
182 PEDRO   As Hector, I assure you, and in the managing of
quarrels you may say he is wise, for either he avoids
them with great discretion, or undertakes them with a
most Christianlike fear.
LEONATO   If he do fear God, a must necessarily keep
peace. If he break the peace, he ought to enter into a
quarrel with fear and trembling.
PEDRO   And so will he do, for the man doth fear God,
190   howsoever it seems not in him by some large jests he
will make. Well, I am sorry for your niece. Shall we go
seek Benedick and tell him of her love?
CLAUDIO   Never tell him, my lord. Let her wear it out
194   with good counsel.
LEONATO   Nay, that's impossible; she may wear her heart
out first.
PEDRO   Well, we will hear further of it by your daughter.
Let it cool the while. I love Benedick well, and I could
wish he would modestly examine himself to see how
200   much he is unworthy so good a lady.
LEONATO   My lord, will you walk? Dinner is ready.
CLAUDIO   *[Aside]* If he do not dote on her upon this, I
will never trust my expectation.
PEDRO   *[Aside]* Let there be the same net spread for her,
205   and that must your daughter and her gentlewomen carry.

---

173 *tender* offer   175 *contemptible* contemptuous   176 *proper* handsome
177 *outward happiness* attractive exterior   180 *wit* intelligence   182 *Hector*
the most valiant Trojan   190 *by* to judge by   194 *counsel* reflection   205
carry manage

The sport will be, when they hold one an opinion of   206
another's dotage, and no such matter. That's the scene
that I would see, which will be merely a dumb show.   208
Let us send her to call him in to dinner.

   [Exeunt Don Pedro, Claudio, and Leonato.]

BENEDICK   *[Advancing]* This can be no trick. The con-   210
ference was sadly borne; they have the truth of this   211
from Hero; they seem to pity the lady. It seems her
affections have their full bent. Love me? Why, it must   213
be requited. I hear how I am censured. They say I will
bear myself proudly if I perceive the love come from her.
They say too that she will rather die than give any sign of
affection. I did never think to marry. I must not seem
proud. Happy are they that hear their detractions and   218
can put them to mending. They say the lady is fair – 'tis
a truth, I can bear them witness; and virtuous – 'tis so, I   220
cannot reprove it; and wise, but for loving me – by my   221
troth, it is no addition to her wit, nor no great argument
of her folly, for I will be horribly in love with her. I may
chance have some odd quirks and remnants of wit bro-   224
ken on me because I have railed so long against marriage.
But doth not the appetite alter? A man loves the meat in
his youth that he cannot endure in his age. Shall quips
and sentences and these paper bullets of the brain awe a   228
man from the career of his humor? No, the world must   229
be peopled. When I said I would die a bachelor, I did not   230
think I should live till I were married. Here comes Beatrice.   *Enter Beatrice.* By this day, she's a fair lady! I do
spy some marks of love in her.

BEATRICE   Against my will I am sent to bid you come in
to dinner.

206–7 *they . . . dotage* each thinks the other is in love   208 *dumb show* pan-
tomime (because they can no longer carry on their usual banter)   211 *sadly
borne* seriously carried on   213 *affections . . . bent* emotions are like a bow
fully bent   218 *their detractions* themselves criticized   221 *reprove* disprove
224 *quirks* quips, quibbles   228 *sentences* maxims, wise sayings; *paper bullets*
words; *awe* frighten   229 *career of his humor* action he fancies

BENEDICK   Fair Beatrice, I thank you for your pains.

BEATRICE   I took no more pains for those thanks than
you take pains to thank me. If it had been painful, I
would not have come.

240 BENEDICK   You take pleasure then in the message?

BEATRICE   Yea, just so much as you may take upon a
242   knife's point, and choke a daw withal. You have no
243   stomach, signor? Fare you well.   *Exit.*

BENEDICK   Ha! "Against my will I am sent to bid you
come in to dinner." There's a double meaning in that.
"I took no more pains for those thanks than you took
pains to thank me." That's as much as to say, "Any
pains that I take for you is as easy as thanks." If I do not
take pity of her, I am a villain; if I do not love her, I am
250   a Jew. I will go get her picture.   *Exit.*

*

~ **III.1** *Enter Hero and two Gentlewomen, Margaret
and Ursula.*

HERO
Good Margaret, run thee to the parlor.
There shalt thou find my cousin Beatrice
3   Proposing with the prince and Claudio.
Whisper her ear and tell her I and Ursley
Walk in the orchard, and our whole discourse
Is all of her. Say that thou overheard'st us,
7   And bid her steal into the pleachèd bower,
8   Where honeysuckles, ripened by the sun,
Forbid the sun to enter – like favorites,
10   Made proud by princes, that advance their pride
Against that power that bred it. There will she hide her

---

242 *daw withal* jackdaw with   243 *stomach* appetite   250 *Jew* (Elizabethan
stereotype of lack of Christian charity)
   III.1 Leonato's garden   3 *Proposing* conversing   7 *pleachèd* hidden by
thickly interwoven branches   8 *ripened* brought to full development

To listen our propose. This is thy office.   12
Bear thee well in it and leave us alone.   13

MARGARET
I'll make her come, I warrant you, presently.   *[Exit.]*   14

HERO
Now, Ursula, when Beatrice doth come,
As we do trace this alley up and down,   16
Our talk must only be of Benedick.
When I do name him, let it be thy part
To praise him more than ever man did merit.
My talk to thee must be how Benedick   20
Is sick in love with Beatrice. Of this matter
Is little Cupid's crafty arrow made,
That only wounds by hearsay.
       Enter Beatrice [and hides].   Now begin,
For look where Beatrice like a lapwing runs   24
Close by the ground, to hear our conference.

URSULA
The pleasant'st angling is to see the fish
Cut with her golden oars the silver stream   27
And greedily devour the treacherous bait.
So angle we for Beatrice, who even now
Is couchèd in the woodbine coverture.   30
Fear you not my part of the dialogue.

HERO
Then go we near her, that her ear lose nothing
Of the false sweet bait that we lay for it.
       [They move to where Beatrice is hiding.]
No, truly, Ursula, she is too disdainful.
I know her spirits are as coy and wild   35
As haggards of the rock.   36

URSULA   But are you sure
That Benedick loves Beatrice so entirely?

---

12 *propose* conversation   13 *leave us alone* leave the rest to us   14 *presently*
immediately   16 *trace* walk along   24 *lapwing* kind of plover   27 *oars* i.e.,
fins   30 *couchèd* hidden; *woodbine* honeysuckle; *coverture* arbor   35 *coy* disdainful   36 *haggards* untamed mature female hawks

HERO
  So says the prince, and my new-trothèd lord.

URSULA
  And did they bid you tell her of it, madam?

HERO
40 They did entreat me to acquaint her of it,
  But I persuaded them, if they loved Benedick,
  To wish him wrestle with affection
  And never to let Beatrice know of it.

URSULA
  Why did you so? Doth not the gentleman
45 Deserve as full as fortunate a bed
  As ever Beatrice shall couch upon?

HERO
  O god of love! I know he doth deserve
  As much as may be yielded to a man.
  But nature never framed a woman's heart
50 Of prouder stuff than that of Beatrice.
  Disdain and scorn ride sparkling in her eyes,
52 Misprizing what they look on, and her wit
  Values itself so highly that to her
  All matter else seems weak. She cannot love,
55 Nor take no shape nor project of affection,
  She is so self-endeared.

URSULA   Sure I think so,
  And therefore certainly it were not good
  She knew his love, lest she'll make sport at it.

HERO
  Why, you speak truth. I never yet saw man,
60 How wise, how noble, young, how rarely featured,
61 But she would spell him backward. If fair-faced,
  She would swear the gentleman should be her sister;
63 If black, why, nature, drawing of an antic,

---

45 *as full* fully 52 *Misprizing* undervaluing, mistaking 55 *project* idea, notion 61 *spell him backward* turn him inside out 63 *black* dark-complexioned; *antic* grotesque figure, buffoon

Made a foul blot; if tall, a lance ill-headed;
If low, an agate very vilely cut;   65
If speaking, why, a vane blown with all winds;   66
If silent, why, a block movèd with none.
So turns she every man the wrong side out
And never gives to truth and virtue that
Which simpleness and merit purchaseth.   70

URSULA
Sure, sure, such carping is not commendable.   71

HERO
No, not to be so odd, and from all fashions,   72
As Beatrice is, cannot be commendable.
But who dare tell her so? If I should speak,
She would mock me into air, O, she would laugh me
Out of myself, press me to death with wit!   76
Therefore let Benedick, like covered fire,
Consume away in sighs, waste inwardly.   78
It were a better death than die with mocks,
Which is as bad as die with tickling.   80

URSULA
Yet tell her of it. Hear what she will say.

HERO
No, rather I will go to Benedick
And counsel him to fight against his passion.
And truly, I'll devise some honest slanders   84
To stain my cousin with. One doth not know
How much an ill word may empoison liking.

URSULA
O, do not do your cousin such a wrong!
She cannot be so much without true judgment

---

65 *agate* figure carved on an agate and so very small   66 *vane* weather vane;
with by   70 *simpleness* plain sincerity   71 *carping* faultfinding   72 *from*
contrary to   76 *press me to death* (The usual penalty in England for refusing
to plead guilty or not guilty. Weights were piled on the victim's body until he
either pleaded or died.)   78 *Consume . . . sighs* (since each sigh was held to
cost the heart a drop of blood)   84 *honest slanders* adverse criticisms, but not
of such a nature as to impugn her honesty (i.e., her chastity)

(Having so swift and excellent a wit
90 As she is prized to have) as to refuse
So rare a gentleman as Signor Benedick.

HERO
He is the only man of Italy,
Always excepted my dear Claudio.

URSULA
I pray you be not angry with me, madam,
Speaking my fancy: Signor Benedick,
96 For shape, for bearing, argument, and valor,
Goes foremost in report through Italy.

HERO
Indeed he hath an excellent good name.

URSULA
His excellence did earn it ere he had it.
100 When are you married, madam?

HERO
101 Why, every day tomorrow! Come, go in.
I'll show thee some attires, and have thy counsel
103 Which is the best to furnish me tomorrow.

URSULA   *[Aside]*
104 She's limed, I warrant you! We have caught her, madam.

HERO   *[Aside]*
105 If it prove so, then loving goes by haps.
Some Cupid kills with arrows, some with traps.
                              [Exeunt Hero and Ursula.]

BEATRICE   *[Coming forward]*
107 What fire is in mine ears? Can this be true?
Stand I condemned for pride and scorn so much?
Contempt, farewell! and maiden pride, adieu!
110 No glory lives behind the back of such.
And, Benedick, love on, I will requite thee,

---

90 *prized* esteemed   **96** *bearing* deportment; *argument* discourse   **101** *every day tomorrow* tomorrow and forever after   **103** *furnish* dress   **104** *limed* caught as with birdlime   **105** *haps* chance   **107** *What . . . ears* how my ears burn   **110** *No . . . such* the proud and contemptuous are never praised except to their faces

Taming my wild heart to thy loving hand.   112
If thou dost love, my kindness shall incite thee
    To bind our loves up in a holy band,
For others say thou dost deserve, and I
Believe it better than reportingly.   *Exit.*   116

                          *

∾ **III.2** *Enter Prince [Don Pedro], Claudio, Benedick,
    and Leonato.*

PEDRO   I do but stay till your marriage be consummate,
    and then go I toward Aragon.
CLAUDIO   I'll bring you thither, my lord, if you'll vouch- 3
    safe me.
PEDRO   Nay, that would be as great a soil in the new gloss
    of your marriage as to show a child his new coat and
    forbid him to wear it. I will only be bold with Benedick 7
    for his company, for, from the crown of his head to the
    sole of his foot, he is all mirth. He hath twice or thrice
    cut Cupid's bowstring, and the little hangman dare not 10
    shoot at him. He hath a heart as sound as a bell, and his
    tongue is the clapper, for what his heart thinks, his
    tongue speaks.
BENEDICK   Gallants, I am not as I have been.
LEONATO   So say I. Methinks you are sadder.   15
CLAUDIO   I hope he be in love.
PEDRO   Hang him, truant! There's no true drop of blood   17
    in him to be truly touched with love. If he be sad, he
    wants money.
BENEDICK   I have the toothache.   20
PEDRO   Draw it.   21
BENEDICK   Hang it!

---

112 *Taming . . . hand* (the hawk figure again) 116 *better than reportingly*
not merely as hearsay
    III.2 3–4 *vouchsafe* permit **7** *be bold with* ask **10** *hangman* execu-
tioner, rogue **15** *sadder* more serious **17** *truant* (from love) **20** *toothache*
(supposed to be common among lovers) **21** *Draw* extract (but with punning reference below to the hanging, drawing, and quartering of traitors)

CLAUDIO   You must hang it first and draw it afterwards.

PEDRO   What? sigh for the toothache?

25 LEONATO   Where is but a humor or a worm.

26 BENEDICK   Well, everyone can master a grief but he that has it.

CLAUDIO   Yet say I he is in love.

29 PEDRO   There is no appearance of fancy in him, unless it
30 be a fancy that he hath to strange disguises, as to be a Dutchman today, a Frenchman tomorrow, or in the shape of two countries at once, as a German from the
33 waist downward, all slops, and a Spaniard from the hip
34 upward, no doublet. Unless he have a fancy to this fool-
35 ery, as it appears he hath, he is no fool for fancy, as you would have it appear he is.

CLAUDIO   If he be not in love with some woman, there is no believing old signs. A brushes his hat o' mornings. What should that bode?

40 PEDRO   Hath any man seen him at the barber's?

CLAUDIO   No, but the barber's man hath been seen with
42 him, and the old ornament of his cheek hath already stuffed tennis balls.

LEONATO   Indeed he looks younger than he did, by the loss of a beard.

46 PEDRO   Nay, a rubs himself with civet. Can you smell him out by that?

CLAUDIO   That's as much as to say, the sweet youth's in love.

50 PEDRO   The greatest note of it is his melancholy.

51 CLAUDIO   And when was he wont to wash his face?

---

25 *humor* one of the four bodily fluids, in this case rheum; *worm* (supposed to cause toothache)   26 *grief* physical as well as mental pain   29–30 *fancy . . . fancy* love . . . whim   30 *strange disguises* (the Englishman's dress was a perennial joke)   33 *slops* loose breeches   34 *no doublet* (wearing a short Spanish cloak over his doublet)   35 *fool for fancy* i.e., lover   42–43 *ornament . . . balls* i.e., his beard has been shaved (tennis balls were stuffed with curled hair)   46 *civet* (a popular perfume)   46–47 *smell him out* (1) smell him, (2) work out his secret   51 *wash his face* apply cosmetics

PEDRO   Yea, or to paint himself? for the which I hear
what they say of him.

CLAUDIO   Nay, but his jesting spirit, which is now crept
into a lute string, and now governed by stops.   55

PEDRO   Indeed that tells a heavy tale for him. Conclude,
conclude, he is in love.

CLAUDIO   Nay, but I know who loves him.

PEDRO   That would I know too. I warrant, one that
knows him not.   60

CLAUDIO   Yes, and his ill conditions, and in despite of   61
all, dies for him.   62

PEDRO   She shall be buried with her face upwards.   63

BENEDICK   Yet is this no charm for the toothache. Old   64
signor, walk aside with me. I have studied eight or nine
wise words to speak to you, which these hobbyhorses   66
must not hear.   *[Exeunt Benedick and Leonato.]*

PEDRO   For my life, to break with him about Beatrice!   68

CLAUDIO   'Tis even so. Hero and Margaret have by this
played their parts with Beatrice, and then the two bears   70
will not bite one another when they meet.

        Enter John the Bastard.

JOHN   My lord and brother, God save you.

PEDRO   Good den, brother.   73

JOHN   If your leisure served, I would speak with you.

PEDRO   In private?

JOHN   If it please you. Yet Count Claudio may hear, for
what I would speak of concerns him.

PEDRO   What's the matter?

JOHN   *[To Claudio]* Means your lordship to be married
tomorrow?   80

---

55 *stops* fingerings, or positions, marked for the fingers on the fingerboard
of a lute, the lover's instrument   61 *ill conditions* bad qualities   62
dies . . . him (punning on "die" as "have an orgasm")   63 *face upwards* (because she will have "died," had an orgasm, when on her back under Benedick
during intercourse)   64 *charm* i.e., cure; *Old* (a term of respect)   66 *hobbyhorses* buffoons (originally an antic figure in a morris dance)   68 *For my life*
upon my life   73 *Good den* good evening

PEDRO   You know he does.

JOHN   I know not that, when he knows what I know.

CLAUDIO   If there be any impediment, I pray you
84   discover it.

JOHN   You may think I love you not. Let that appear
86   hereafter, and aim better at me by that I now will man-
      ifest. For my brother, I think he holds you well and in
88   dearness of heart hath holp to effect your ensuing mar-
      riage – surely suit ill spent and labor ill bestowed!

90 PEDRO   Why, what's the matter?

91 JOHN   I came hither to tell you, and, circumstances
92   shortened (for she has been too long a-talking of), the
93   lady is disloyal.

CLAUDIO   Who? Hero?

JOHN   Even she – Leonato's Hero, your Hero, every
      man's Hero.

CLAUDIO   Disloyal?

98 JOHN   The word is too good to paint out her wickedness.
      I could say she were worse; think you of a worse title,
100   and I will fit her to it. Wonder not till further warrant.
      Go but with me tonight, you shall see her chamber
      window entered, even the night before her wedding
      day. If you love her then, tomorrow wed her. But it
      would better fit your honor to change your mind.

CLAUDIO   May this be so?

PEDRO   I will not think it.

107 JOHN   If you dare not trust that you see, confess not that
      you know. If you will follow me, I will show you
      enough; and when you have seen more and heard
110   more, proceed accordingly.

CLAUDIO   If I see anything tonight why I should not
112   marry her tomorrow, in the congregation where I
      should wed there will I shame her.

---

84 *discover* disclose   86 *aim . . . me* judge better of me   88 *dearness of heart*
friendship;   *holp* helped   91–92 *circumstances shortened* circumstantial details omitted   92 *a-talking of* talked of   93 *disloyal* unfaithful   98 *paint out*
portray   100 *till further warrant* till further assured by proof   107 *that* what
112 *congregation* company

PEDRO   And, as I wooed for thee to obtain her, I will join
with thee to disgrace her.

JOHN   I will disparage her no farther till you are my wit-
nesses. Bear it coldly but till midnight, and let the issue   117
show itself.

PEDRO   O day untowardly turned!   119

CLAUDIO   O mischief strangely thwarting!   120

JOHN   O plague right well prevented!   121
So will you say when you have seen the sequel.

[Exeunt.]

*

⌒ **III.3**   *Enter Dogberry and his compartner [Verges],*
with the Watch.   [handwritten: played by clown who played
Bottom / buffoons]

[handwritten: marked this way originally]

DOGBERRY   Are you good men and true?

VERGES   Yea, or else it were pity but they should suffer
salvation, body and soul.   3

DOGBERRY   Nay, that were a punishment too good for
them if they should have any allegiance in them, being   5
chosen for the prince's watch.   6

VERGES   Well, give them their charge, neighbor Dog-   7
berry.

DOGBERRY   First, who think you the most desertless man   9
to be constable?   10

FIRST WATCHMAN   Hugh Oatcake, sir, or George Seacoal,
for they can write and read.

---

117 *coldly* coolly   119 *untowardly* unfavorably, unluckily   121 *plague* mis-
fortune; *prevented* forestalled

III.3 A street in Messina **s.d.** *Dogberry* (from the shrub dogwood); *Verges*
(probably from "verge," a staff of office); *Watch* (Exactly how many watchmen there are [at least three] and who speaks which lines are unclear; the
speech prefix is often simply *Watch,* suggesting Shakespeare might have left it
to the actors to decide who spoke which lines. I have kept to Q's speech prefixes except at 88, 96, and 106, which I have assigned to the Second Watchman, George Seacoal, who is the leader of the watch.)   3 *salvation* (his
mistake for "damnation")   5 *allegiance* (for "treachery")   6 *watch* men chosen to police the streets at night   7 *charge* orders   9 *desertless* (for "deserv-
ing")   10 *constable* deputy leader of the watch (Dogberry is the *right master
constable,* III.3.164)

DOGBERRY   Come hither, neighbor Seacoal. God hath
14   blessed you with a good name. To be a well-favored
man is the gift of fortune, but to write and read comes
by nature.

SECOND WATCHMAN [GEORGE SEACOAL]   Both which,
master constable –

DOGBERRY   You have. I knew it would be your answer.
20   Well, for your favor, sir, why, give God thanks and
make no boast of it, and for your writing and reading,
let that appear when there is no need of such vanity.
23   You are thought here to be the most senseless and fit
man for the constable of the watch. Therefore bear you
25   the lantern. This is your charge: you shall comprehend
26   all vagrom men; you are to bid any man stand, in the
prince's name.

SECOND WATCHMAN   How if a will not stand?

DOGBERRY   Why then, take no note of him, but let him
30   go, and presently call the rest of the watch together and
thank God you are rid of a knave.

VERGES   If he will not stand when he is bidden, he is
none of the prince's subjects.

DOGBERRY   True, and they are to meddle with none but
the prince's subjects. You shall also make no noise in
the streets, for, for the watch to babble and to talk is
37   most tolerable, and not to be endured.

A WATCHMAN   We will rather sleep than talk. We know
39   what belongs to a watch.

40   DOGBERRY   Why, you speak like an ancient and most
quiet watchman, for I cannot see how sleeping should
42   offend. Only have a care that your bills be not stolen.
Well, you are to call at all the alehouses and bid those
that are drunk get them to bed.

---

14 *well-favored* handsome   20 *favor* appearance   23 *senseless* (for "sensible")
25 *comprehend* (for "apprehend")   26 *vagrom* vagrant   37 *tolerable* (for "in-
tolerable")   39 *belongs to* is the duty of   40 *ancient* elderly, staid   42 *bills*
halberds (long poles with combination ax and spear heads carried chiefly as a
badge of office)

A WATCHMAN   How if they will not?

DOGBERRY   Why then, let them alone till they are sober.
If they make you not then the better answer, you may
say they are not the men you took them for.

A WATCHMAN   Well, sir.

DOGBERRY   If you meet a thief, you may suspect him, by   50
virtue of your office, to be no true man, and for such   51
kind of men, the less you meddle or make with them,   52
why, the more is for your honesty.   53

A WATCHMAN   If we know him to be a thief, shall we not
lay hands on him?

DOGBERRY   Truly, by your office you may, but I think
they that touch pitch will be defiled. The most peace-   57
able way for you, if you do take a thief, is to let him
show himself what he is, and steal out of your company.   60

VERGES   You have been always called a merciful man,
partner.

DOGBERRY   Truly, I would not hang a dog by my will,
much more a man who hath any honesty in him.   64

VERGES   If you hear a child cry in the night, you must
call to the nurse and bid her still it.

A WATCHMAN   How if the nurse be asleep and will not
hear us?

DOGBERRY   Why then, depart in peace and let the child
wake her with crying, for the ewe that will not hear her   70
lamb when it baas will never answer a calf when he   71
bleats.

VERGES   'Tis very true.

DOGBERRY   This is the end of the charge: you, constable,
are to present the prince's own person. If you meet the   75
prince in the night, you may stay him.

---

51 *true* honest   52 *meddle or make* associate   53 *the more is* the better it is
57 *they ... defiled* (paraphrased from Ecclesiasticus 13:1)   64 *more* (for
"less")   71 *calf* (Dogberry's comparison has led him to call the watchman a
calf, or dolt)   75 *present* represent

77 VERGES Nay, by'r Lady, that I think a cannot.

DOGBERRY Five shillings to one on't with any man that
79 knows the statutes, he may stay him! Marry, not with-
80 out the prince be willing; for indeed the watch ought to
81 offend no man, and it is an offense to stay a man
against his will.

VERGES By'r Lady, I think it be so.

84 DOGBERRY Ha, ah, ha! Well, masters, good night. An
there be any matter of weight chances, call up me. Keep
your fellows' counsels and your own, and good night.
[To Verges] Come, neighbor.

SECOND WATCHMAN Well, masters, we hear our charge.
Let us go sit here upon the church bench till two, and
90 then all to bed.

DOGBERRY One word more, honest neighbors. I pray
you watch about Signor Leonato's door, for the wed-
93 ding being there tomorrow, there is a great coil tonight.
94 Adieu. Be vigitant, I beseech you.

Exeunt [Dogberry and Verges].
Enter Borachio and Conrad.

BORACHIO What, Conrad!

SECOND WATCHMAN *[Aside]* Peace! stir not!

BORACHIO Conrad, I say!

CONRAD Here, man. I am at thy elbow.

99 BORACHIO Mass, and my elbow itched! I thought there
100 would a scab follow.

101 CONRAD I will owe thee an answer for that, and now
forward with thy tale.

---

77 *by'r Lady* by Our Lady (a mild oath)   **79** *statutes* acts of Parliament (but
the principle actually belongs to common law)   **81** *offense* (in the legal
sense)   **84** *Ha, ah, ha* (a laugh of triumph)   **93** *coil* bustle   **94** *vigitant* (for
"vigilant")   **99** *Mass* (a mild interjection; originally, by the mass)   **100** *scab*
i.e., an itching scab, with play on slang term for a scurvy fellow   **101** *owe*
thee an answer answer that later

BORACHIO   Stand thee close then under this penthouse, 103
for it drizzles rain, and I will, like a true drunkard, utter 104
all to thee.

SECOND WATCHMAN   *[Aside]* Some treason, masters. Yet
stand close.

BORACHIO   Therefore know I have earned of Don John a
thousand ducats.

CONRAD   Is it possible that any villainy should be so 110
dear? 111

BORACHIO   Thou shouldst rather ask if it were possible
any villainy should be so rich, for when rich villains
have need of poor ones, poor ones may make what
price they will.

CONRAD   I wonder at it.

BORACHIO   That shows thou art unconfirmed. Thou 117
knowest that the fashion of a doublet, or a hat, or a
cloak, is nothing to a man.

CONRAD   Yes, it is apparel. 120

BORACHIO   I mean the fashion.

CONRAD   Yes, the fashion is the fashion.

BORACHIO   Tush! I may as well say the fool's the fool.
But seest thou not what a deformed thief this fashion 124
is?

A WATCHMAN   *[Aside]* I know that Deformed. A has been
a vile thief this seven year; a goes up and down like a 127
gentleman. I remember his name.

BORACHIO   Didst thou not hear somebody?

CONRAD   No, 'twas the vane on the house. 130

BORACHIO   Seest thou not, I say, what a deformed thief
this fashion is? how giddily a turns about all the hot-
bloods between fourteen and five-and-thirty? sometimes fashioning them like Pharaoh's soldiers in the

---

103 *penthouse* overhanging roof   104 *true drunkard* (punning on his name,
since *borrachón* is Spanish for "drunkard," and there was a proverb, "The
drunkard tells all")   111 *dear* expensive   117 *unconfirmed* inexperienced
124 *deformed thief* deforming rascal   127 *goes up and down* walks about
130 *vane* weather vane

135   reechy painting, sometime like god Bel's priests in the
136   old church window, sometime like the shaven Hercules
        in the smirched worm-eaten tapestry, where his
138   codpiece seems as massy as his club?
        CONRAD   All this I see, and I see that the fashion wears
140   out more apparel than the man. But art not thou thy-
        self giddy with the fashion too, that thou hast shifted
        out of thy tale into telling me of the fashion?
        BORACHIO   Not so neither. But know that I have tonight
        wooed Margaret, the Lady Hero's gentlewoman, by the
        name of Hero. She leans me out at her mistress' chamber
        window, bids me a thousand times good night – I tell
        this tale vilely. I should first tell thee how the prince,
148   Claudio, and my master, planted and placed and pos-
        sessed by my master Don John, saw afar off in the or-
150   chard this amiable encounter.
        CONRAD   And thought they Margaret was Hero?
        BORACHIO   Two of them did, the prince and Claudio,
        but the devil my master knew she was Margaret, and
        partly by his oaths, which first possessed them, partly
        by the dark night, which did deceive them, but chiefly
        by my villainy, which did confirm any slander that Don
        John had made, away went Claudio enraged, swore he
        would meet her, as he was appointed, next morning at
        the temple, and there, before the whole congregation,
160   shame her with what he saw o'ernight and send her
        home again without a husband.
        FIRST WATCHMAN   We charge you in the prince's name,
        stand!
        SECOND WATCHMAN   Call up the right master constable.
165   We have here recovered the most dangerous piece of
        lechery that ever was known in the commonwealth.

---

135 *reechy* grimy, smoky; *Bel's priests* the priests of Baal (in the Apocryphal book of the Bible Bel and the Dragon)   **136** *shaven Hercules* (probably a confusion with Samson, whose hair was cut by Delilah)   **138** *codpiece* front part of breeches, often stuffed and ornamented   **148–49** *possessed* deluded **150** *amiable encounter* lovers' meeting   **165** *recovered* (for "discovered"); *lechery* (for "treachery")

FIRST WATCHMAN   And one Deformed is one of them. I
     know him; a wears a lock.   168
CONRAD   Masters, masters —
SECOND WATCHMAN   You'll be made bring Deformed   170
     forth, I warrant you.
CONRAD   Masters —
A WATCHMAN   Never speak, we charge you. Let us obey   173
     you to go with us.
BORACHIO   We are like to prove a goodly commodity,   175
     being taken up of these men's bills.   176
CONRAD   A commodity in question, I warrant you.   177
     Come, we'll obey you.   *Exeunt.*

                              ✳

∾ **III.4** *Enter Hero, and Margaret and Ursula.*

HERO   Good Ursula, wake my cousin Beatrice and desire
     her to rise.
URSULA   I will, lady.
HERO   And bid her come hither.
URSULA   Well.   *[Exit.]*
MARGARET   Troth, I think your other rebato were better.   6
HERO   No, pray thee, good Meg, I'll wear this.
MARGARET   By my troth 's not so good, and I warrant
     your cousin will say so.
HERO   My cousin's a fool, and thou art another. I'll wear   10
     none but this.
MARGARET   I like the new tire within excellently, if the   12
     hair were a thought browner; and your gown's a most
     rare fashion, i' faith. I saw the Duchess of Milan's gown
     that they praise so.

---

168 *lock* lovelock (a wisp of hair worn beside the left ear, often down to the
shoulder)   **173–74** *Let us obey you* (for "we command you")   **175** *commodity* merchandise   **176** *taken up* (1) arrested, (2) obtained on credit from a
usurer; *bills* (1) halberds, (2) bonds of goods   **177** *in question* (1) subject to
examination, (2) of doubtful quality
     III.4 The house of Leonato   **6** *rebato* stiff, flaring collar or ruff, usually of
starched or wired lace   **12** *tire* headdress with wig and elaborate ornaments
attached; *within* in the next room

HERO   O, that exceeds, they say.

17 MARGARET   By my troth, 's but a nightgown in respect of
18   yours – cloth a gold and cuts, and laced with silver, set
19   with pearls, down sleeves, side sleeves, and skirts,
20   round underborne with a bluish tinsel. But for a fine,
21   quaint, graceful, and excellent fashion, yours is worth
   ten on't.

HERO   God give me joy to wear it! for my heart is exceeding heavy.

MARGARET   'Twill be heavier soon by the weight of a
   man.

HERO   Fie upon thee! art not ashamed?

MARGARET   Of what, lady? of speaking honorably? Is not
29   marriage honorable in a beggar? Is not your lord honor-
30   able without marriage? I think you would have me say,
31   "saving your reverence, a husband." An bad thinking
32   do not wrest true speaking, I'll offend nobody. Is there
   any harm in "the heavier for a husband"? None, I
   think, an it be the right husband and the right wife.
35   Otherwise 'tis light, and not heavy. Ask my Lady Beat-
36   rice else. Here she comes.
     Enter Beatrice.

37 HERO   Good morrow, coz.

BEATRICE   Good morrow, sweet Hero.

HERO   Why, how now? Do you speak in the sick tune?

40 BEATRICE   I am out of all other tune, methinks.

41 MARGARET   Clap's into "Light a love." That goes without
42   a burden. Do you sing it, and I'll dance it.

---

17 *nightgown* dressing gown   18 *cuts* slashes or notches to show the under-
body; *laced with silver* with silver threads applied, usually in a diagonal pat-
tern   19 *down sleeves* close-fitting long sleeves; *side sleeves* second, purely
ornamental, sleeves hanging open from the armhole   20 *round underborne*
held out, stiffened from underneath   21 *quaint* elegant   29 *in* even in   31
saving your reverence (conventional apology for mentioning a delicate subject)   32 *wrest* twist, misunderstand   35 *light* (pun on "wanton")   36 *else* if
it be otherwise   37 *coz* cousin   41 *Clap's into* let us begin briskly; "*Light a
love*" (an old tune)   42 *burden* refrain (with a punning reference to *heavier
for a husband*)

BEATRICE   Ye light a love with your heels! then, if your   43
husband have stables enough, you'll see he shall lack no
barns.   45

MARGARET   O illegitimate construction! I scorn that
with my heels.

BEATRICE   'Tis almost five o'clock, cousin, 'tis time you
were ready. By my troth, I am exceeding ill. Heigh-ho!

MARGARET   For a hawk, a horse, or a husband?   50

BEATRICE   For the letter that begins them all, H.   51

MARGARET   Well, an you be not turned Turk, there's no   52
more sailing by the star.   53

BEATRICE   What means the fool, trow?   54

MARGARET   Nothing I, but God send everyone their
heart's desire!

HERO   These gloves the count sent me, they are an excellent perfume.   58

BEATRICE   I am stuffed, cousin, I cannot smell.   59

MARGARET   A maid, and stuffed! There's goodly catching   60
of cold.

BEATRICE   O, God help me, God help me! How long
have you professed apprehension?   63

MARGARET   Ever since you left it. Doth not my wit become me rarely?   65

BEATRICE   It is not seen enough. You should wear it in   66
your cap. By my troth, I am sick.

MARGARET   Get you some of this distilled *Carduus bene-*   68
dictus and lay it to your heart. It is the only thing for a
qualm.   70

---

43 *light . . . heels* i.e., grow wanton   **45** *barns* (punning on "bairns," children)   **50** (treating Beatrice's sigh as a hunting cry)   **51** *H* (with a play on
"ache," then pronounced "aitch")   **52** *turned Turk* i.e., turned renegade,
changed your vow   **53** *star* North Star   **54** *trow* I wonder   **58** *perfume*
(gloves were often perfumed)   **59** *I am stuffed* i.e., my nose is stopped with a
cold   **60** *stuffed* pregnant   **63** *professed apprehension* pretended to wit   **65**
rarely excellently   **66–67** *in your cap* (like a feather, where it would show)
68–69 *Carduus benedictus* holy thistle (regarded as a universal remedy, with
pun on "Benedick")   **70** *qualm* sudden faintness or nausea

71 HERO   There thou prick'st her with a thistle.

BEATRICE   *Benedictus*? why *benedictus*? You have some
73   moral in this *benedictus*.

MARGARET   Moral? No, by my troth, I have no moral
meaning. I meant plain holy thistle. You may think
perchance that I think you are in love. Nay, by'r Lady, I
77   am not such a fool to think what I list, nor I list not to
think what I can, nor indeed I cannot think, if I would
think my heart out of thinking, that you are in love, or
80   that you will be in love, or that you can be in love. Yet
81   Benedick was such another, and now is he become a
man. He swore he would never marry, and yet now in
83   despite of his heart he eats his meat without grudging –
and how you may be converted I know not, but methinks you look with your eyes as other women do.

BEATRICE   What pace is this that thy tongue keeps?
87 MARGARET   Not a false gallop.

    Enter Ursula.

URSULA   Madam, withdraw. The prince, the count,
Signor Benedick, Don John, and all the gallants of the
90   town are come to fetch you to church.

HERO   Help to dress me, good coz, good Meg, good
Ursula.   *[Exeunt.]*

                            *

    ～ III.5   *Enter Leonato and the Constable [Dogberry]*
        and the Headborough [Verges].

LEONATO   What would you with me, honest neighbor?
2 DOGBERRY   Marry, sir, I would have some confidence
3   with you that decerns you nearly.

LEONATO   Brief, I pray you, for you see it is a busy time
with me.

---

71 *prick'st* (with pun on "penis")   73 *moral* figurative meaning   77 *list* like,
please   81–82 *a man* i.e., a normal man   83 *eats . . . grudging* has a normal
appetite   87 *false gallop* canter, but the emphasis is on "false"
    III.5 s.d. *Headborough* petty or local constable   2 *confidence* (for "confer-
ence")   3 *decerns* (for "concerns")

DOGBERRY   Marry, this it is, sir.

VERGES   Yes, in truth it is, sir.

LEONATO   What is it, my good friends?

DOGBERRY   Goodman Verges, sir, speaks a little off the
matter – an old man, sir, and his wits are not so blunt   10
as, God help, I would desire they were, but, in faith,
honest as the skin between his brows.   12

VERGES   Yes, I thank God I am as honest as any man living that is an old man and no honester than I.

DOGBERRY   Comparisons are odorous. *Palabras*, neigh-   15
bor Verges.

LEONATO   Neighbors, you are tedious.

DOGBERRY   It pleases your worship to say so, but we are
the poor duke's officers; but truly, for mine own part, if   19
I were as tedious as a king, I could find in my heart to   20
bestow it all of your worship.

LEONATO   All thy tediousness on me, ah?

DOGBERRY   Yea, an 'twere a thousand pound more than
'tis, for I hear as good exclamation on your worship as   24
of any man in the city, and though I be but a poor man,
I am glad to hear it.

VERGES   And so am I.

LEONATO   I would fain know what you have to say.

VERGES   Marry, sir, our watch tonight, excepting your   29
worship's presence, ha' ta'en a couple of as arrant knaves   30
as any in Messina.

DOGBERRY   A good old man, sir, he will be talking. As   32
they say, "When the age is in, the wit is out." God help
us, it is a world to see! Well said, i' faith, neighbor
Verges. Well, God's a good man. An two men ride of a
horse, one must ride behind. An honest soul, i' faith,
sir, by my troth he is, as ever broke bread, but God is to

---

10 *blunt* (for "sharp")   12 *honest . . . brows* (proverbial)   15 *odorous* (for
"odious"); *Palabras* (from Spanish *pocas palabras*, few words)   19 *poor duke's*
(for "duke's poor")   24 *exclamation* (for "acclamation")   29 *excepting* (for
"respecting")   32 ff. *As they say*, etc. (what follows is a string of "old ends,"
or stock phrases)

be worshiped, all men are not alike, alas, good neighbor!

40 LEONATO   Indeed, neighbor, he comes too short of you.

DOGBERRY   Gifts that God gives.

LEONATO   I must leave you.

DOGBERRY   One word, sir. Our watch, sir, have indeed
44   comprehended two aspicious persons, and we would
have them this morning examined before your worship.

LEONATO   Take their examination yourself and bring it
me. I am now in great haste, as it may appear unto you.

49 DOGBERRY   It shall be suffigance.

50 LEONATO   Drink some wine ere you go. Fare you well.
    [Enter a Messenger.]

MESSENGER   My lord, they stay for you to give your
daughter to her husband.

LEONATO   I'll wait upon them. I am ready.
                        [Exeunt Leonato and Messenger.]

54 DOGBERRY   Go, good partner, go get you to Francis Seacoal. Bid him bring his pen and inkhorn to the jail. We
56   are now to examination these men.

VERGES   And we must do it wisely.

DOGBERRY   We will spare for no wit, I warrant you.
59   Here's that shall drive some of them to a noncome.
60   Only get the learned writer to set down our excom-
munication, and meet me at the jail.   *[Exeunt.]*

*

～ **IV.1**   *Enter Prince [Don Pedro], [John the] Bastard,
Leonato, Friar [Francis], Claudio, Benedick, Hero,
and Beatrice.*

---

44 *comprehended* (for "apprehended"); *aspicious* (for "suspicious")   49 *suffigance* (for "sufficient")   54–55 *Francis Seacoal* (the sexton or town clerk of
IV.2, not the same as George Seacoal, constable of the watch, in III.3, who
could read and write)   56 *examination* (for "examine")   59 *noncome* (abbre-
viation of *non compos mentis*, but he probably means "nonplus")   60–61 *ex-
communication* (for "examination")

   IV.1 A church   **s.d.** (editors often add entries for servants and wedding
guests)

LEONATO   Come, Friar Francis, be brief. Only to the
plain form of marriage, and you shall recount their par-   2
ticular duties afterwards.

FRIAR   You come hither, my lord, to marry this lady?

CLAUDIO   No.

LEONATO   To be married to her. Friar, you come to
marry her.

FRIAR   Lady, you come hither to be married to this
count?

HERO   I do.   10

FRIAR   If either of you know any inward impediment   11
why you should not be conjoined, I charge you on your
souls to utter it.

CLAUDIO   Know you any, Hero?

HERO   None, my lord.

FRIAR   Know you any, count?

LEONATO   I dare make his answer – none.

CLAUDIO   O, what men dare do! what men may do! what
men daily do, not knowing what they do!

BENEDICK   How now? interjections? Why then, some be   20
of laughing, as, ah, ha, he!

CLAUDIO
Stand thee by, friar. Father, by your leave,   22
Will you with free and unconstrainèd soul
Give me this maid your daughter?

LEONATO
As freely, son, as God did give her me.

CLAUDIO
And what have I to give you back whose worth
May counterpoise this rich and precious gift?   27

PEDRO
Nothing, unless you render her again.

---

2 *plain form* simple prescribed formula   2–3 *particular duties* the usual pre-
liminary sermon on the duties of husband and wife   11 *inward impediment*
secret, or mental, reservation   20–21 *some . . . ah, ha, he* (he is quoting Lily's
Latin Grammar, a standard textbook of the day, which says of interjections,
"Some are of Laughing: as, Ha, ha, he.")   22 *Stand thee by* stand aside; *by
your leave* if I may call you so   27 *counterpoise* balance

CLAUDIO

29   Sweet prince, you learn me noble thankfulness.

30   There, Leonato, take her back again.

     Give not this rotten orange to your friend.

32   She's but the sign and semblance of her honor.

     Behold how like a maid she blushes here!

34   O, what authority and show of truth

35   Can cunning sin cover itself withal!

36   Comes not that blood as modest evidence

37   To witness simple virtue? Would you not swear,

     All you that see her, that she were a maid,

     By these exterior shows? But she is none:

40   She knows the heat of a luxurious bed;

     Her blush is guiltiness, not modesty.

LEONATO

     What do you mean, my lord?

CLAUDIO   Not to be married,

43   Not to knit my soul to an approvèd wanton.

LEONATO

44   Dear my lord, if you, in your own proof,

     Have vanquished the resistance of her youth

     And made defeat of her virginity –

CLAUDIO

     I know what you would say. If I have known her,

     You will say she did embrace me as a husband,

49   And so extenuate the forehand sin.

50   No, Leonato,

51   I never tempted her with word too large,

     But, as a brother to his sister, showed

     Bashful sincerity and comely love.

HERO

     And seemed I ever otherwise to you?

---

29 *Sweet* dear; *learn* teach **32** *sign* appearance **34** *authority* assurance **35** *withal* with **36** *blood* blush **37** *witness* bear witness to **40** *luxurious* lustful **43** *approvèd* proved **44** *proof* experience **49** *extenuate . . . sin* excuse the sin of anticipating the marriage state **51** *large* broad, immodest

CLAUDIO
　Out on thee seeming! I will write against it.　　　55
　You seem to me as Dian in her orb,　　　56
　As chaste as is the bud ere it be blown,　　　57
　But you are more intemperate in your blood　　　58
　Than Venus, or those pampered animals
　That rage in savage sensuality.　　　60
HERO
　Is my lord well that he doth speak so wide?　　　61
LEONATO
　Sweet prince, why speak not you?
PEDRO　　　　　　　　　　　　What should I speak?
　I stand dishonored that have gone about　　　63
　To link my dear friend to a common stale.　　　64
LEONATO
　Are these things spoken, or do I but dream?
JOHN
　Sir, they are spoken, and these things are true.
BENEDICK
　This looks not like a nuptial.
HERO　　　　　　　　　　　　"True"! O God!
CLAUDIO
　Leonato, stand I here?
　Is this the prince? Is this the prince's brother?
　Is this face Hero's? Are our eyes our own?　　　70
LEONATO
　All this is so; but what of this, my lord?
CLAUDIO
　Let me but move one question to your daughter,
　And by that fatherly and kindly power　　　73
　That you have in her, bid her answer truly.
LEONATO
　I charge thee do so, as thou art my child.

---

55 *Out* shame　56 *Dian* Diana, goddess of chastity; *orb* sphere, the moon
57 *blown* in blossom　58 *intemperate* ungoverned　61 *wide* far from the
truth　63 *gone about* undertaken　64 *stale* prostitute　73 *kindly* natural

HERO

O, God defend me! How am I beset!
What kind of catechizing call you this?

CLAUDIO

To make you answer truly to your name.

HERO

Is it not Hero? Who can blot that name
80 With any just reproach?

CLAUDIO   Marry, that can Hero!
81 Hero itself can blot out Hero's virtue.
What man was he talked with you yesternight,
Out at your window betwixt twelve and one?
84 Now, if you are a maid, answer to this.

HERO

I talked with no man at that hour, my lord.

PEDRO

Why, then are you no maiden. Leonato,
I am sorry you must hear. Upon mine honor
88 Myself, my brother, and this grievèd count
Did see her, hear her, at that hour last night
90 Talk with a ruffian at her chamber window,
91 Who hath indeed, most like a liberal villain,
Confessed the vile encounters they have had
A thousand times in secret.

JOHN

Fie, fie! they are not to be named, my lord –
Not to be spoke of;
There is not chastity enough in language
Without offense to utter them. Thus, pretty lady,
98 I am sorry for thy much misgovernment.

CLAUDIO

O Hero! what a Hero hadst thou been
100 If half thy outward graces had been placed

---

81 *Hero itself* i.e., the name by which he had heard Borachio call Margaret
84 *answer to* explain   88 *grievèd* aggrieved, wronged   91 *liberal* licentious
98 *much misgovernment* great misconduct

About thy thoughts and counsels of thy heart!
But fare thee well, most foul, most fair! Farewell,
Thou pure impiety and impious purity!
For thee I'll lock up all the gates of love,
And on my eyelids shall conjecture hang,   105
To turn all beauty into thoughts of harm,
And never shall it more be gracious.

LEONATO
Hath no man's dagger here a point for me?
    [Hero swoons.]

BEATRICE
Why, how now, cousin? Wherefore sink you down?

JOHN
Come let us go. These things, come thus to light,   *110*
Smother her spirits up.   111
        [Exeunt Don Pedro, Don John, and Claudio.]

BENEDICK
How doth the lady?

BEATRICE   Dead, I think. Help, uncle!
Hero! why, Hero! Uncle! Signor Benedick! Friar!

LEONATO
O Fate, take not away thy heavy hand!
Death is the fairest cover for her shame
That may be wished for.

BEATRICE   How now, cousin Hero?

FRIAR   Have comfort, lady.

LEONATO   Dost thou look up?   118

FRIAR   Yea, wherefore should she not?

LEONATO
Wherefore? Why, doth not every earthly thing   *120*
Cry shame upon her? Could she here deny
The story that is printed in her blood?   122
Do not live, Hero, do not ope thine eyes,
For, did I think thou wouldst not quickly die,

---

105 *conjecture* doubt, suspicion   111 *spirits* vital powers   118 *look up* (a
sign of innocence)   122 *printed in her blood* written in her blushes

Thought I thy spirits were stronger than thy shames,
126   Myself would on the rearward of reproaches
Strike at thy life. Grieved I, I had but one?
128   Chid I for that at frugal nature's frame?
O, one too much by thee! Why had I one?
130   Why ever wast thou lovely in my eyes?
Why had I not with charitable hand
Took up a beggar's issue at my gates,
Who smirchèd thus and mired with infamy,
I might have said, "No part of it is mine;
This shame derives itself from unknown loins"?
But mine, and mine I loved, and mine I praised,
And mine that I was proud on – mine so much
138   That I myself was to myself not mine,
Valuing of her – why she, O, she is fall'n
140   Into a pit of ink, that the wide sea
Hath drops too few to wash her clean again,
142   And salt too little which may season give
To her foul tainted flesh!

BENEDICK   Sir, sir, be patient.
For my part, I am so attired in wonder,
I know not what to say.

BEATRICE
O, on my soul, my cousin is belied!

BENEDICK
Lady, were you her bedfellow last night?

BEATRICE
No, truly not, although, until last night,
I have this twelvemonth been her bedfellow.

LEONATO
150   Confirmed, confirmed! O, that is stronger made
Which was before barred up with ribs of iron!
Would the two princes lie? and Claudio lie,

---

126 *on . . . reproaches* after reproaching you   128 *frame* plan, design   138 *I myself . . . mine* I lost or forgot myself   142 *season give* provide a preservative

Who loved her so that, speaking of her foulness,
Washed it with tears? Hence from her! let her die.

FRIAR
  Hear me a little;
  For I have only been silent so long,
  And given way unto this course of fortune,   157
  By noting of the lady. I have marked
  A thousand blushing apparitions   159
  To start into her face, a thousand innocent shames   160
  In angel whiteness beat away those blushes,
  And in her eye there hath appeared a fire
  To burn the errors that these princes hold   163
  Against her maiden truth. Call me a fool,
  Trust not my reading nor my observations,
  Which with experimental seal doth warrant   166
  The tenor of my book, trust not my age,
  My reverence, calling, nor divinity,
  If this sweet lady lie not guiltless here
  Under some biting error.   170

LEONATO   Friar, it cannot be.
  Thou seest that all the grace that she hath left
  Is that she will not add to her damnation
  A sin of perjury: she not denies it.
  Why seek'st thou then to cover with excuse
  That which appears in proper nakedness?

FRIAR
  Lady, what man is he you are accused of?

HERO
  They know that do accuse me; I know none.
  If I know more of any man alive
  Than that which maiden modesty doth warrant,
  Let all my sins lack mercy! O my father,   180

---

157 *course of fortune* turn of events   159 *blushing apparitions* blushes (personified)   163 *errors* (personified as heretics)   166 *experimental seal* seal of
experience   166–67 *warrant . . . book* confirm the tone of my philosophy

Prove you that any man with me conversed
182 At hours unmeet, or that I yesternight
183 Maintained the change of words with any creature,
184 Refuse me, hate me, torture me to death!

FRIAR
185 There is some strange misprision in the princes.

BENEDICK
186 Two of them have the very bent of honor;
     And if their wisdoms be misled in this,
188 The practice of it lives in John the Bastard,
189 Whose spirits toil in frame of villainies.

LEONATO
190 I know not. If they speak but truth of her,
     These hands shall tear her. If they wrong her honor,
     The proudest of them shall well hear of it.
     Time hath not yet so dried this blood of mine,
194 Nor age so eat up my invention,
     Nor fortune made such havoc of my means,
     Nor my bad life reft me so much of friends,
197 But they shall find awaked in such a kind
198 Both strength of limb and policy of mind,
     Ability in means, and choice of friends,
200 To quit me of them throughly.

FRIAR   Pause awhile
     And let my counsel sway you in this case.
202 Your daughter here the princess (left for dead),
203 Let her awhile be secretly kept in,
     And publish it that she is dead indeed,
205 Maintain a mourning ostentation,

---

182 *unmeet* improper   183 *Maintained* carried on; *change* exchange   184
Refuse disown   185 *misprision* mistake   186 *bent* shape, form   188 *practice*
plotting   189 *in frame of* in framing   194 *invention* power to make plans
197 *kind* manner   198 *policy of mind* mental power   200 *quit me of* settle
accounts with; *throughly* thoroughly   202 *princess* (So in quarto and folio
texts, although Hero is not, in this version of the story, a princess. Perhaps a
courtesy title, or perhaps an author's inconsistency; often emended to
"princes left for dead.")   203 *in* at home   205 *mourning ostentation* formal
show of mourning

And on your family's old monument
Hang mournful epitaphs, and do all rites
That appertain unto a burial.

LEONATO

What shall become of this? What will this do?

FRIAR

Marry, this well carried shall on her behalf　　　　210
Change slander to remorse. That is some good.
But not for that dream I on this strange course,
But on this travail look for greater birth.　　　　213
She dying, as it must be so maintained,
Upon the instant that she was accused,
Shall be lamented, pitied, and excused
Of every hearer; for it so falls out
That what we have we prize not to the worth　　　218
Whiles we enjoy it, but being lacked and lost,
Why, then we rack the value, then we find　　　　220
The virtue that possession would not show us
Whiles it was ours. So will it fare with Claudio.
When he shall hear she died upon his words,
Th' idea of her life shall sweetly creep　　　　224
Into his study of imagination,　　　　　　　　225
And every lovely organ of her life　　　　　　226
Shall come appareled in more precious habit,　　227
More moving, delicate, and full of life,
Into the eye and prospect of his soul
Than when she lived indeed. Then shall he mourn　　*230*
(If ever love had interest in his liver)　　　　231
And wish he had not so accusèd her –
No, though he thought his accusation true.
Let this be so, and doubt not but success　　　　234

---

210 *carried* managed　**213** *on this travail* as a result of this effort　**218** *to the worth* for what it is worth　**220** *rack* stretch as on a torture rack　**224** *idea . . . life* i.e., memory of her　**225** *his . . . imagination* the thoughts of his musing hours　**226** *organ of her life* part of her when she was alive　**227** *habit* apparel　**231** *liver* (the presumed physiological seat of love, in contrast to the heart, the romantic seat)　**234** *success* what succeeds or follows (i.e., the course of time)

235 Will fashion the event in better shape
Than I can lay it down in likelihood.
237 But if all aim but this be leveled false,
The supposition of the lady's death
Will quench the wonder of her infamy.
240 And if it sort not well, you may conceal her,
As best befits her wounded reputation,
242 In some reclusive and religious life,
Out of all eyes, tongues, minds, and injuries.

BENEDICK
Signor Leonato, let the friar advise you,
245 And though you know my inwardness and love
Is very much unto the prince and Claudio,
Yet, by mine honor, I will deal in this
As secretly and justly as your soul
249 Should with your body.

LEONATO   Being that I flow in grief,
250 The smallest twine may lead me.

FRIAR
'Tis well consented. Presently away,
252 For to strange sores strangely they strain the cure.
Come, lady, die to live. This wedding day
254 Perhaps is but prolonged. Have patience and endure.
                    Exit [with all but Beatrice and Benedick].

BENEDICK   Lady Beatrice, have you wept all this while?
BEATRICE   Yea, and I will weep a while longer.
BENEDICK   I will not desire that.
BEATRICE   You have no reason. I do it freely.
BENEDICK   Surely I do believe your fair cousin is
260   wronged.
BEATRICE   Ah, how much might the man deserve of me
that would right her!
BENEDICK   Is there any way to show such friendship?

---

235 *event* outcome   237 *be leveled false* be directed falsely (and so miss the
mark)   240 *sort* turn out   242 *reclusive* cloistered   245 *inwardness* intimacy
249 *flow* am afloat (and hence easily pulled)   252 *strain the cure* i.e., use desperate remedies   254 *prolonged* deferred

BEATRICE   A very even way, but no such friend.   264
BENEDICK   May a man do it?
BEATRICE   It is a man's office, but not yours.
BENEDICK   I do love nothing in the world so well as you.
   Is not that strange?
BEATRICE   As strange as the thing I know not. It were as
   possible for me to say I loved nothing so well as you.   270
   But believe me not – and yet I lie not. I confess noth-
   ing, nor I deny nothing. I am sorry for my cousin.
BENEDICK   By my sword, Beatrice, thou lovest me.
BEATRICE   Do not swear and eat it.   274
BENEDICK   I will swear by it that you love me, and I will
   make him eat it that says I love not you.
BEATRICE   Will you not eat your word?
BENEDICK   With no sauce that can be devised to it. I
   protest I love thee.   279
BEATRICE   Why then, God forgive me!   280
BENEDICK   What offense, sweet Beatrice?
BEATRICE   You have stayed me in a happy hour. I was   282
   about to protest I loved you.
BENEDICK   And do it with all thy heart.
BEATRICE   I love you with so much of my heart that none
   is left to protest.
BENEDICK   Come, bid me do anything for thee.
BEATRICE   Kill Claudio.
BENEDICK   Ha! not for the wide world!
BEATRICE   You kill me to deny it. Farewell.   290
BENEDICK   Tarry, sweet Beatrice.
BEATRICE   I am gone, though I am here. There is no love
   in you. Nay, I pray you let me go.
BENEDICK   Beatrice –
BEATRICE   In faith, I will go.
BENEDICK   We'll be friends first.
BEATRICE   You dare easier be friends with me than fight
   with mine enemy.

---

264 *even* direct   274 *swear and eat it* i.e., eat the words of this oath, go back
on it   279 *protest* solemnly affirm   282 *stayed* stopped

BENEDICK   Is Claudio thine enemy?

300 BEATRICE   Is a not approved in the height a villain, that
hath slandered, scorned, dishonored my kinswoman?
302 O that I were a man! What? bear her in hand until they
303 come to take hands, and then with public accusation,
304 uncovered slander, unmitigated rancor – O God, that I
were a man! I would eat his heart in the marketplace.

BENEDICK   Hear me, Beatrice –

BEATRICE   Talk with a man out at a window! – a proper
saying!

BENEDICK   Nay, but Beatrice –

310 BEATRICE   Sweet Hero! she is wronged, she is slandered,
311 she is undone.

BENEDICK   Beat –

313 BEATRICE   Princes and counties! Surely a princely testi-
314 mony, a goodly count, Count Comfit, a sweet gallant
surely! O that I were a man for his sake! or that I had
any friend would be a man for my sake! But manhood
is melted into curtsies, valor into compliment, and
men are only turned into tongue, and trim ones too.
He is now as valiant as Hercules that only tells a lie, and
320 swears it. I cannot be a man with wishing, therefore I
will die a woman with grieving.

BENEDICK   Tarry, good Beatrice. By this hand, I love
thee.

BEATRICE   Use it for my love some other way than swear-
ing by it.

BENEDICK   Think you in your soul the Count Claudio
hath wronged Hero?

BEATRICE   Yea, as sure as I have a thought or a soul.

BENEDICK   Enough, I am engaged. I will challenge him.
330 I will kiss your hand, and so I leave you. By this hand,
Claudio shall render me a dear account. As you hear of

---

300 *approved* proved; *height* highest degree   302 *bear her in hand* lead her
on, delude her   303 *take hands* marry   304 *uncovered* undisguised   311
undone ruined   313 *Counties* counts   314 *count* legal indictment and account (with a pun on Claudio's title); *Comfit* comfit, sugar candy

me, so think of me. Go comfort your cousin. I must say
she is dead – and so farewell.   *[Exeunt.]*

*

∾ **IV.2** *Enter the Constables [Dogberry and Verges] and
the Town Clerk [Sexton] in gowns, Borachio [, Conrad,
and Watch].*

DOGBERRY   Is our whole dissembly appeared?   1
VERGES   O, a stool and a cushion for the sexton.
SEXTON   Which be the malefactors?
DOGBERRY   Marry, that am I and my partner.
VERGES   Nay, that's certain. We have the exhibition to   5
examine.
SEXTON   But which are the offenders that are to be ex-
amined? Let them come before master constable.
DOGBERRY   Yea, marry, let them come before me. What
is your name, friend?   10
BORACHIO   Borachio.
DOGBERRY   Pray write down Borachio. Yours, sirrah?   12
CONRAD   I am a gentleman, sir, and my name is Conrad.
DOGBERRY   Write down Master Gentleman Conrad.
Masters, do you serve God?
BOTH   Yea, sir, we hope.
DOGBERRY   Write down that they hope they serve God;
and write God first, for God defend but God should go   18
before such villains! Masters, it is proved already that
you are little better than false knaves, and it will go near   20
to be thought so shortly. How answer you for your-
selves?
CONRAD   Marry, sir, we say we are none.
DOGBERRY   A marvelous witty fellow, I assure you, but I
will go about with him. *[To Borachio]* Come you hither,   25

<hr>

IV.2 (the speech prefixes in Q show that Will Kemp and Richard Cowley
played, or were imagined by Shakespeare as playing, Dogberry and Verges)
1 *dissembly* (for "assembly")   5 *exhibition* (for "commission")   12 *sirrah* sir
(a derogatory form, resented by Conrad)   18 *defend* forbid   25 *go about
with* undertake, deal with

sirrah. A word in your ear. Sir, I say to you, it is thought
you are false knaves.

BORACHIO   Sir, I say to you we are none.

29 DOGBERRY   Well, stand aside. 'Fore God, they are both in
30 a tale. Have you writ down that they are none?

SEXTON   Master constable, you go not the way to examine. You must call forth the watch that are their ac-
cusers.

34 DOGBERRY   Yea, marry, that's the eftest way. Let the
watch come forth. Masters, I charge you in the prince's
name accuse these men.

FIRST WATCHMAN   This man said, sir, that Don John the
prince's brother was a villain.

DOGBERRY   Write down Prince John a villain. Why, this
40 is flat perjury, to call a prince's brother villain.

BORACHIO   Master constable –

DOGBERRY   Pray thee, fellow, peace. I do not like thy
look, I promise thee.

SEXTON   What heard you him say else?

SECOND WATCHMAN   Marry, that he had received a thousand ducats of Don John for accusing the Lady Hero
wrongfully.

DOGBERRY   Flat burglary as ever was committed.

VERGES   Yea, by mass, that it is.

50 SEXTON   What else, fellow?

FIRST WATCHMAN   And that Count Claudio did mean,
upon his words, to disgrace Hero before the whole assembly, and not marry her.

DOGBERRY   O villain! Thou wilt be condemned into
55 everlasting redemption for this.

SEXTON   What else?

WATCHMEN   This is all.

SEXTON   And this is more, masters, than you can deny.
Prince John is this morning secretly stolen away. Hero

———
29–30 *they . . . tale* both tell the same story   34 *eftest* easiest, quickest   55
redemption (for "damnation")

was in this manner accused, in this very manner re- 60
fused, and upon the grief of this suddenly died. Master
constable, let these men be bound and brought to
Leonato's. I will go before and show him their examination.   *[Exit.]*

DOGBERRY   Come, let them be opinioned.   65

VERGES   Let them be in the hands –

CONRAD   Off, coxcomb!   67

DOGBERRY   God's my life, where's the sexton? Let him
write down the prince's officer coxcomb. Come, bind
them. – Thou naughty varlet!   70

CONRAD   Away! you are an ass, you are an ass.

DOGBERRY   Dost thou not suspect my place? Dost thou   72
not suspect my years? O that he were here to write me
down an ass! But, masters, remember that I am an ass.
Though it be not written down, yet forget not that I
am an ass. No, thou villain, thou art full of piety, as 76
shall be proved upon thee by good witness. I am a wise
fellow; and which is more, an officer; and which is
more, a householder; and which is more, as pretty a
piece of flesh as any is in Messina, and one that knows 80
the law, go to! and a rich fellow enough, go to! and a
fellow that hath had losses; and one that hath two   82
gowns and everything handsome about him. Bring him
away. O that I had been writ down an ass!

Exit [with the others].

.*

∾ **V.1** *Enter Leonato and his brother [Antonio].*

ANTONIO
If you go on thus, you will kill yourself,

---

65 *opinioned* (for "pinioned")   **67** (the speech could belong to Borachio);
coxcomb fool (derived from the comb of red flannel worn on the head of a
professional court jester)   **70** *naughty* wicked; *varlet* scoundrel   **72** *suspect*
(for "respect")   **76** *piety* (for "impiety")   **82** *had losses* (implying that he had
had possessions to lose)

2   And 'tis not wisdom thus to second grief
     Against yourself.
     LEONATO   I pray thee cease thy counsel,
     Which falls into mine ears as profitless
     As water in a sieve. Give not me counsel,
     Nor let no comforter delight mine ear
7   But such a one whose wrongs do suit with mine.
     Bring me a father that so loved his child,
9   Whose joy of her is overwhelmed like mine,
10   And bid him speak of patience.
     Measure his woe the length and breadth of mine,
12   And let it answer every strain for strain,
     As thus for thus, and such a grief for such,
     In every lineament, branch, shape, and form.
15   If such a one will smile and stroke his beard,
16   Bid sorrow wag, cry "hem" when he should groan,
     Patch grief with proverbs, make misfortune drunk
18   With candlewasters – bring him yet to me,
     And I of him will gather patience.
20   But there is no such man, for, brother, men
     Can counsel and speak comfort to that grief
     Which they themselves not feel, but, tasting it,
     Their counsel turns to passion, which before
24   Would give preceptial medicine to rage,
     Fetter strong madness in a silken thread,
26   Charm ache with air and agony with words.
     No, no! 'Tis all men's office to speak patience
28   To those that wring under the load of sorrow,
     But no man's virtue nor sufficiency
30   To be so moral when he shall endure
     The like himself. Therefore give me no counsel.
32   My griefs cry louder than advertisement.

V.1 2 *second* support, assist   7 *suit with* match   9 *overwhelmed* drowned, as
with tears   12 *strain* trait   15 *stroke his beard* (a gesture of complacency)
16 *wag* go away   18 *candlewasters* i.e., moral philosophers or carousers   24
preceptial medicine remedy in the form of precepts   26 *Charm . . . air* allay
pain with talk   28 *wring* writhe   32 *advertisement* advice

ANTONIO
  Therein do men from children nothing differ.
LEONATO
  I pray thee peace. I will be flesh and blood;
  For there was never yet philosopher
  That could endure the toothache patiently,
  However they have writ the style of gods   37
  And made a pish at chance and sufferance.   38
ANTONIO
  Yet bend not all the harm upon yourself.
  Make those that do offend you suffer too.   40
LEONATO
  There thou speak'st reason. Nay, I will do so.
  My soul doth tell me Hero is belied,
  And that shall Claudio know, so shall the prince,
  And all of them that thus dishonor her.
    Enter Prince [Don Pedro] and Claudio.
ANTONIO
  Here comes the prince and Claudio hastily.
PEDRO
  Good den, good den.   46
CLAUDIO   Good day to both of you.
LEONATO
  Hear you, my lords –
PEDRO   We have some haste, Leonato.
LEONATO
  Some haste, my lord! well, fare you well, my lord.
  Are you so hasty now? Well, all is one.   49
PEDRO
  Nay, do not quarrel with us, good old man.   50
ANTONIO
  If he could right himself with quarreling,
  Some of us would lie low.   52

---

37 *writ* written in   38 *made a pish* scoffed; *chance* mischance; *sufferance* suffering   46 *Good den* good evening   49 *all is one* it does not matter   52 *Some of us* i.e., Don Pedro and Claudio

CLAUDIO   Who wrongs him?

LEONATO

53   Marry, thou dost wrong me, thou dissembler, thou!

Nay, never lay thy hand upon thy sword;

55   I fear thee not.

CLAUDIO   Marry, beshrew my hand

If it should give your age such cause of fear.

In faith, my hand meant nothing to my sword.

LEONATO

58   Tush, tush, man! never fleer and jest at me.

I speak not like a dotard nor a fool,

60   As under privilege of age to brag

What I have done being young, or what would do,

Were I not old. Know, Claudio, to thy head,

Thou hast so wronged mine innocent child and me

64   That I am forced to lay my reverence by

65   And, with gray hairs and bruise of many days,

66   Do challenge thee to trial of a man.

I say thou hast belied mine innocent child.

Thy slander hath gone through and through her heart,

And she lies buried with her ancestors –

70   O, in a tomb where never scandal slept,

71   Save this of hers, framed by thy villainy!

CLAUDIO

My villainy?

LEONATO   Thine, Claudio, thine I say.

PEDRO

You say not right, old man.

LEONATO   My lord, my lord,

I'll prove it on his body if he dare,

75   Despite his nice fence and his active practice,

76   His May of youth and bloom of lustihood.

---

53 *thou* (distinguished from the more respectful "you" with which he addresses the prince)   55 *beshrew* (mild curse)   58 *fleer* jeer   64 *lay . . . by* renounce the respect due to old age   65 *bruise* wear and tear   66 *trial of a man* manly trial (i.e., a duel)   71 *framed* made   75 *nice fence* clever swordplay   76 *lustihood* vigor, strength

CLAUDIO
Away! I will not have to do with you.
LEONATO
Canst thou so doff me? Thou hast killed my child.   78
If thou kill'st me, boy, thou shalt kill a man.
ANTONIO
He shall kill two of us, and men indeed.   80
But that's no matter, let him kill one first.
Win me and wear me! Let him answer me.   82
Come, follow me, boy. Come, sir boy, come follow
    me.
Sir boy, I'll whip you from your foining fence!   84
Nay, as I am a gentleman, I will.
LEONATO
Brother –
ANTONIO
Content yourself. God knows I loved my niece,   87
And she is dead, slandered to death by villains,
That dare as well answer a man indeed
As I dare take a serpent by the tongue.   90
Boys, apes, braggarts, jacks, milksops!   91
LEONATO   Brother Antony –
ANTONIO
Hold you content. What, man! I know them, yea,
And what they weigh, even to the utmost scruple,   93
Scambling, outfacing, fashionmonging boys,   94
That lie and cog and flout, deprave and slander,   95
Go anticly and show an outward hideousness,   96
And speak off half a dozen dangerous words,
How they might hurt their enemies, if they durst;
And this is all.

---

78 *doff* put aside   82 *Win . . . wear me* (a proverb, serving as a form of challenge)   84 *foining* thrusting   87 *Content* calm   91 *jacks* knaves   93 *scruple* smallest measure of weight   94 *Scambling* quarrelsome; *outfacing* impudent; *fashionmonging* fashionmongering   95 *cog* cheat; *flout* jeer at; *deprave* defame   96 *anticly* fantastically dressed; *hideousness* frightening aspect

LEONATO

100 But, brother Antony –

ANTONIO   Come, 'tis no matter.
Do not you meddle, let me deal in this.

PEDRO

102 Gentlemen both, we will not wake your patience.
My heart is sorry for your daughter's death,
But, on my honor, she was charged with nothing

105 But what was true, and very full of proof.

LEONATO
My lord, my lord –

PEDRO
I will not hear you.

LEONATO
No? Come, brother, away! – I will be heard.

ANTONIO

109 And shall, or some of us will smart for it. *Exeunt ambo.*
Enter Benedick.

110 PEDRO   See, see! Here comes the man we went to seek.

CLAUDIO   Now, signor, what news?

BENEDICK   Good day, my lord.

113 PEDRO   Welcome, signor. You are almost come to part almost a fray.

CLAUDIO   We had liked to have had our two noses
snapped off with two old men without teeth.

PEDRO   Leonato and his brother. What think'st thou?

118 Had we fought, I doubt we should have been too
young for them.

120 BENEDICK   In a false quarrel there is no true valor. I came
to seek you both.

CLAUDIO   We have been up and down to seek thee; for

123 we are high-proof melancholy, and would fain have it
beaten away. Wilt thou use thy wit?

BENEDICK   It is in my scabbard. Shall I draw it?

---

102 *wake your patience* cause you to need patience   105 *full of proof* fully
proved   109 s.d. *ambo* both (Leonato and Antonio)   113 *almost come* come
almost in time   118 *doubt* suspect   123 *high-proof* in a high degree

PEDRO   Dost thou wear thy wit by thy side?

CLAUDIO   Never any did so, though very many have
been beside their wit. I will bid thee draw, as we do the   128
minstrels – draw to pleasure us.

PEDRO   As I am an honest man, he looks pale. Art thou   130
sick, or angry?

CLAUDIO   What, courage, man! What though care killed
a cat, thou hast mettle enough in thee to kill care.   133

BENEDICK   Sir, I shall meet your wit in the career an you   134
charge it against me. I pray you choose another subject.

CLAUDIO   Nay then, give him another staff; this last was
broke cross.   137

PEDRO   By this light, he changes more and more. I think
he be angry indeed.

CLAUDIO   If he be, he knows how to turn his girdle.   140

BENEDICK   Shall I speak a word in your ear?

CLAUDIO   God bless me from a challenge!

BENEDICK   *[Aside to Claudio]* You are a villain. I jest not;
I will make it good how you dare, with what you dare,
and when you dare. Do me right, or I will protest your   145
cowardice. You have killed a sweet lady, and her death
shall fall heavy on you. Let me hear from you.

CLAUDIO   Well, I will meet you, so I may have good
cheer.

PEDRO   What, a feast? a feast?   150

CLAUDIO   I' faith, I thank him, he hath bid me to a calf's   151
head and a capon, the which if I do not carve most cu-   152
riously, say my knife's naught. Shall I not find a wood-   153
cock too?

BENEDICK   Sir, your wit ambles well; it goes easily.

---

128 *beside their wit* out of their minds; *draw* (used of a sword, and of a min-
strel's bow)   133 *mettle* vivacity   134 *in the career* while running at full
speed   134–35 *an you charge it* if you charge with it (as with a lance in a tilt)
137 *broke cross* broken across (as by an unskillful tilter)   140 *turn his girdle*
prepare for a bout   145 *Do me right* accept my challenge; *protest* report
abroad   151 *bid* invited; *calf's* i.e., fool's   152 *capon* a castrated cock
152–53 *curiously* expertly   153 *naught* good for nothing 153–54 *woodcock*
bird famous for its stupidity

156 PEDRO I'll tell thee how Beatrice praised thy wit the
157   other day. I said thou hadst a fine wit: "True," said she,
    "a fine little one." "No," said I, "a great wit." "Right,"
    says she, "a great gross one." "Nay," said I, "a good wit."
160   "Just," said she, "it hurts nobody." "Nay," said I, "the
161   gentleman is wise." "Certain," said she, "a wise gentle-
162   man." "Nay," said I, "he hath the tongues." "That I be-
    lieve," said she, "for he swore a thing to me on Monday
164   night which he forswore on Tuesday morning. There's a
    double tongue; there's two tongues." Thus did she an
166   hour together transshape thy particular virtues. Yet at
167   last she concluded with a sigh, thou wast the properest
    man in Italy.

   CLAUDIO For the which she wept heartily and said she
170   cared not.

   PEDRO Yea, that she did; but yet, for all that, an if she
    did not hate him deadly, she would love him dearly.
    The old man's daughter told us all.

174 CLAUDIO All, all! And moreover, God saw him when he
    was hid in the garden.

176 PEDRO But when shall we set the savage bull's horns on
    the sensible Benedick's head?

178 CLAUDIO Yea, and text underneath, "Here dwells
    Benedick, the married man"?

180 BENEDICK Fare you well, boy; you know my mind. I will
    leave you now to your gossiplike humor. You break jests
    as braggarts do their blades, which God be thanked
    hurt not. *[To the Prince]* My lord, for your many cour-
    tesies I thank you. I must discontinue your company.
    Your brother the bastard is fled from Messina. You have
    among you killed a sweet and innocent lady. For my
    Lord Lackbeard there, he and I shall meet, and till then
    peace be with him.   *[Exit.]*

---

156 *praised* appraised   157 *fine* excellent, also small   161–62 *wise gentleman* wiseacre   162 *hath the tongues* can speak several languages   164 *forswore* denied   166 *transshape* transform   167 *properest* handsomest   174
God saw him (alluding to Genesis 3:8, but also to the hoaxing of Benedick)
176 *the savage bull's horns* (see I.1.248 ff.)   178 *text* in capital letters

PEDRO   He is in earnest.

CLAUDIO   In most profound earnest, and, I'll warrant *190*
you, for the love of Beatrice.

PEDRO   And hath challenged thee?

CLAUDIO   Most sincerely.

PEDRO   What a pretty thing man is when he goes in his *194*
doublet and hose and leaves off his wit!

> *Enter Constables [Dogberry and Verges, with the*
> *Watch, leading] Conrad and Borachio.*

CLAUDIO   He is then a giant to an ape, but then is an ape *196*
a doctor to such a man.

PEDRO   But, soft you, let me be! Pluck up, my heart, and *198*
be sad! Did he not say my brother was fled?

DOGBERRY   Come you, sir. If justice cannot tame you, *200*
she shall ne'er weigh more reasons in her balance. Nay, *201*
an you be a cursing hypocrite once, you must be looked
to.

PEDRO   How now, two of my brother's men bound? Borachio one.

CLAUDIO   Hearken after their offense, my lord.

PEDRO   Officers, what offense have these men done?

DOGBERRY   Marry, sir, they have committed false report;
moreover, they have spoken untruths; secondarily, they
are slanders; sixth and lastly, they have belied a lady; *210*
thirdly, they have verified unjust things; and to con- *211*
clude, they are lying knaves.

PEDRO   First, I ask thee what they have done; thirdly, I
ask thee what's their offense; sixth and lastly, why they
are committed; and to conclude, what you lay to their *215*
charge?

CLAUDIO   Rightly reasoned, and in his own division, and *217*
by my troth there's one meaning well suited. *218*

194–95 *in . . . hose* i.e., fully dressed   196–97 *a giant . . . man* much bigger
than an ape, but the ape is much wiser than he   198–99 *Pluck . . . sad* pull
up a moment, my mind, and be serious   201 *balance* scales (symbol of justice)   211 *verified* sworn to   215 *committed* arrested and held for trial   217
division scheme of argument   218 *well suited* provided with several different
suits, or modes of speech

PEDRO   Who have you offended, masters, that you are
220   thus bound to your answer? This learned constable is
       too cunning to be understood. What's your offense?

BORACHIO   Sweet prince, let me go no farther to mine
223   answer. Do you hear me, and let this count kill me. I
       have deceived even your very eyes. What your wisdoms
       could not discover, these shallow fools have brought to
       light, who in the night overheard me confessing to this
227   man, how Don John your brother incensed me to slan-
       der the Lady Hero; how you were brought into the or-
       chard and saw me court Margaret in Hero's garments;
230   how you disgraced her when you should marry her. My
       villainy they have upon record, which I had rather seal
       with my death than repeat over to my shame. The lady
       is dead upon mine and my master's false accusation,
       and briefly, I desire nothing but the reward of a villain.

235 PEDRO   Runs not this speech like iron through your
       blood?

CLAUDIO   I have drunk poison whiles he uttered it.

PEDRO   But did my brother set thee on to this?

239 BORACHIO   Yea, and paid me richly for the practice of it.

PEDRO
240   He is composed and framed of treachery,
       And fled he is upon this villainy.

CLAUDIO
       Sweet Hero, now thy image doth appear
243   In the rare semblance that I loved it first.

244 DOGBERRY   Come, bring away the plaintiffs. By this time
245   our sexton hath reformed Signor Leonato of the matter.
       And, masters, do not forget to specify, when time and
       place shall serve, that I am an ass.

VERGES   Here, here comes Master Signor Leonato, and
       the sexton too.

---

220 *bound to your answer* bound over, indicted   **223** *answer* trial   **227** *incensed* incited   **235** *iron* a sword   **239** *practice* accomplishment   **243** *semblance* likeness   **244** *plaintiffs* (for "defendants")   **245** *reformed* (for "informed")

Enter Leonato, his brother [Antonio], and the Sexton.

LEONATO

Which is the villain? Let me see his eyes,   250
That, when I note another man like him,
I may avoid him. Which of these is he?

BORACHIO

If you would know your wronger, look on me.

LEONATO

Art thou the slave that with thy breath hast killed
Mine innocent child?

BORACHIO   Yea, even I alone.

LEONATO

No, not so, villain! thou beliest thyself.
Here stand a pair of honorable men –
A third is fled – that had a hand in it.
I thank you princes for my daughter's death.
Record it with your high and worthy deeds.   260
'Twas bravely done, if you bethink you of it.   261

CLAUDIO

I know not how to pray your patience;   262
Yet I must speak. Choose your revenge yourself;
Impose me to what penance your invention   264
Can lay upon my sin. Yet sinned I not
But in mistaking.

PEDRO   By my soul, nor I!
And yet, to satisfy this good old man,
I would bend under any heavy weight
That he'll enjoin me to.

LEONATO

I cannot bid you bid my daughter live –   270
That were impossible – but I pray you both,
Possess the people in Messina here   272
How innocent she died, and if your love
Can labor aught in sad invention,
Hang her an epitaph upon her tomb,

---

261 *bethink you of* recall   262 *pray your patience* ask your forgiveness   264
Impose me to impose on me   272 *Possess* inform

And sing it to her bones – sing it tonight.
Tomorrow morning come you to my house,
And since you could not be my son-in-law,
Be yet my nephew. My brother hath a daughter,
280   Almost the copy of my child that's dead,
And she alone is heir to both of us.
282   Give her the right you should have giv'n her cousin,
And so dies my revenge.

CLAUDIO   O noble sir!
Your overkindness doth wring tears from me.
285   I do embrace your offer, and dispose
For henceforth of poor Claudio.

LEONATO
Tomorrow then I will expect your coming;
288   Tonight I take my leave. This naughty man
Shall face to face be brought to Margaret,
290   Who I believe was packed in all this wrong,
Hired to it by your brother.

BORACHIO   No, by my soul, she was not,
Nor knew not what she did when she spoke to me,
But always hath been just and virtuous
In anything that I do know by her.

295 DOGBERRY   Moreover, sir, which indeed is not under
white and black, this plaintiff here, the offender, did
call me ass. I beseech you let it be remembered in his
punishment. And also the watch heard them talk of
299   one Deformed. They say he wears a key in his ear, and
300   a lock hanging by it, and borrows money in God's
name, the which he hath used so long and never paid
that now men grow hardhearted and will lend nothing
for God's sake. Pray you examine him upon that point.

LEONATO   I thank thee for thy care and honest pains.

---

282 *right* right of becoming your wife (perhaps with pun on "rite" of marriage)   285 *dispose* you may dispose   288 *naughty* evil   290 *packed* in the pact, an accomplice   295–96 *under . . . black* in writing   299–300 *key, lock* (his misunderstanding of the *lock* of III.3.168)

DOGBERRY Your worship speaks like a most thankful
and reverent youth, and I praise God for you.

LEONATO   There's for thy pains.
[Gives money.]

DOGBERRY   God save the foundation!   308

LEONATO Go, I discharge thee of thy prisoner, and I   309
thank thee.   310

DOGBERRY   I leave an arrant knave with your worship,
which I beseech your worship to correct yourself, for
the example of others. God keep your worship! I wish
your worship well. God restore you to health! I humbly
give you leave to depart, and if a merry meeting may be 315
wished, God prohibit it! Come, neighbor.   316
                                   [Exeunt Dogberry and Verges.]

LEONATO
Until tomorrow morning, lords, farewell.

ANTONIO
Farewell, my lords. We look for you tomorrow.

PEDRO
We will not fail.

CLAUDIO   Tonight I'll mourn with Hero.
                           [Exeunt Don Pedro and Claudio.]

LEONATO   *[To the Watch]*
Bring you these fellows on. – We'll talk with Margaret,   320
How her acquaintance grew with this lewd fellow.   321
                                                Exeunt.

                             *

❧ **V.2** *Enter Benedick and Margaret [meeting].*

BENEDICK   Pray thee, sweet Mistress Margaret, deserve
well at my hands by helping me to the speech of
Beatrice.

---

308 *God . . . foundation* (conventional phrase used by beggars receiving alms
at the gates of religious or charitable foundations) **309** *discharge* relieve
315 *give you leave* (for "ask your leave") **316** *prohibit* (for "grant") **321**
lewd low, disreputable

MARGARET Will you then write me a sonnet in praise of
my beauty?

6 BENEDICK In so high a style, Margaret, that no man liv-
7 ing shall come over it, for in most comely truth thou
deservest it.

9 MARGARET To have no man come over me? Why, shall I
10 always keep belowstairs?

BENEDICK Thy wit is as quick as the greyhound's
mouth – it catches.

MARGARET And yours as blunt as the fencer's foils,
which hit but hurt not.

BENEDICK A most manly wit, Margaret: it will not hurt
a woman. And so I pray thee call Beatrice. I give thee
17 the bucklers.

18 MARGARET Give us the swords; we have bucklers of our
own.

20 BENEDICK If you use them, Margaret, you must put in
21 the pikes with a vice, and they are dangerous weapons
for maids.

MARGARET Well, I will call Beatrice to you, who I think
hath legs.   *Exit Margaret.*

BENEDICK And therefore will come.

26 *[Sings.]*   The god of love,
                     That sits above
                And knows me, and knows me,
                How pitiful I deserve –

30 I mean in singing; but in loving, Leander the good
31 swimmer, Troilus the first employer of panders, and a

V.2 **6** *style* i.e., of writing, but with a pun on "stile," stairs over a fence **7**
come over outdo **9** *come over* have sex with **10** *keep belowstairs* dwell in the
servants' quarters (i.e., never be mistress of a house by marrying a man of
higher rank) **17** *bucklers* shields **18** *swords* penises; *bucklers* vulvas **21**
pikes spikes in the center of the shields, penises; *vice* screw **26–29** (lines
from a popular song) **30** *Leander* (who swam the Hellespont every night to
see another Hero until he was drowned in a storm) **31** *Troilus* (who was
helped to the love of Cressida by her uncle Pandarus)

whole book full of these quondam carpetmongers, 32
whose names yet run smoothly in the even road of a
blank verse – why, they were never so truly turned over 34
and over as my poor self in love. Marry, I cannot show
it in rhyme. I have tried. I can find out no rhyme to
"lady" but "baby" – an innocent rhyme; for "scorn," 37
"horn" – a hard rhyme; for "school," "fool" – a bab- 38
bling rhyme. Very ominous endings! No, I was not
born under a rhyming planet, nor I cannot woo in 40
festival terms. 41

    Enter Beatrice.

Sweet Beatrice, wouldst thou come when I called thee?

BEATRICE   Yea, signor, and depart when you bid me.

BENEDICK   O, stay but till then!

BEATRICE   "Then" is spoken. Fare you well now. And yet,
ere I go, let me go with that I came for, which is, with
knowing what hath passed between you and Claudio.

BENEDICK   Only foul words, and thereupon I will kiss
thee.

BEATRICE   Foul words is but foul wind, and foul wind is 50
but foul breath, and foul breath is noisome. Therefore I 51
will depart unkissed.

BENEDICK   Thou hast frighted the word out of his right
sense, so forcible is thy wit. But I must tell thee plainly, 54
Claudio undergoes my challenge, and either I must 55
shortly hear from him or I will subscribe him a coward. 56
And I pray thee now tell me, for which of my bad parts
didst thou first fall in love with me?

BEATRICE   For them all together, which maintained so
politic a state of evil that they will not admit any good 60
part to intermingle with them. But for which of my
good parts did you first suffer love for me? 62

---

32 *quondam carpetmongers* ancient carpet knights (i.e., lovers rather than
fighters)   **34–35** *turned over and over* head over heels   **37** *innocent* childish
38 *horn* (punning on a cuckold's horns or an erection)   **41** *festival* elevated
51 *noisome* offensive, bad-smelling   **54** *sense* wits   **55** *undergoes* bears   **56**
subscribe him write him down   **60** *politic* well organized   **62** *suffer* experience, but also feel the pain

BENEDICK   Suffer love! – a good epithet. I do suffer love indeed, for I love thee against my will.

BEATRICE   In spite of your heart, I think. Alas, poor heart! If you spite it for my sake, I will spite it for yours, for I will never love that which my friend hates.

BENEDICK   Thou and I are too wise to woo peaceably.

BEATRICE   It appears not in this confession. There's not
70   one wise man among twenty that will praise himself.

BENEDICK   An old, an old instance, Beatrice, that lived
72   in the time of good neighbors. If a man do not erect in this age his own tomb ere he dies, he shall live no longer in monument than the bell rings and the widow weeps.

BEATRICE   And how long is that, think you?

BENEDICK   Question: why, an hour in clamor and a
78   quarter in rheum. Therefore it is most expedient for the wise, if Don Worm (his conscience) find no impedi-
80   ment to the contrary, to be the trumpet of his own virtues, as I am to myself. So much for praising myself, who, I myself will bear witness, is praiseworthy. And now tell me, how doth your cousin?

BEATRICE   Very ill.

BENEDICK   And how do you?

BEATRICE   Very ill too.

BENEDICK   Serve God, love me, and mend. There will I leave you too, for here comes one in haste.

Enter Ursula.

URSULA   Madam, you must come to your uncle. Yonder's
90   old coil at home. It is proved my Lady Hero hath been falsely accused, the prince and Claudio mightily
92   abused, and Don John is the author of all, who is fled and gone. Will you come presently?

BEATRICE   Will you go hear this news, signor?

95   BENEDICK   I will live in thy heart, die in thy lap, and be

---

72 *time of good neighbors* i.e., golden age   78 *rheum* tears   90 *old coil* confusion   92 *abused* deceived   95 *die in thy lap* (punning on "have an orgasm")

buried in thy eyes, and moreover, I will go with thee to
thy uncle's.   *Exit [with Beatrice and Ursula].*

*

∾ **V.3** *Enter Claudio, Prince [Don Pedro, Lord], and
three or four [Attendants] with tapers [followed by
Musicians].*

CLAUDIO   Is this the monument of Leonato?
LORD   It is, my lord.
CLAUDIO   *[Reads from a scroll.]*

Epitaph.

> Done to death by slanderous tongues   3
>   Was the Hero that here lies.   4
> Death, in guerdon of her wrongs,   5
>   Gives her fame which never dies.
> So the life that died with shame
> Lives in death with glorious fame.

[Hangs up the scroll.]
>   Hang thou there upon the tomb,
>   Praising her when I am dumb.   10
> Now, music, sound, and sing your solemn hymn.   11

Song [by one or more Attendants].

> Pardon, goddess of the night,   12
> Those that slew thy virgin knight,   13
> For the which, with songs of woe,

V.3 s.d. *tapers* candles (as a symbol of penitence)   **3** (Q gives no speech prefix, and the epitaph might well be spoken by the Lord)   **4** *Hero* (pun intended)   **5** *guerdon* reward   **11 s.d.** (perhaps Balthasar is one of the singers)
12 *goddess of the night* Diana, patroness of chastity   **13** *virgin knight* (still
punning on "Hero")

Round about her tomb they go.
Midnight, assist our moan,
Help us to sigh and groan
   Heavily, heavily.
Graves, yawn and yield your dead,
20 ·Till death be utterèd
   Heavily, heavily.

CLAUDIO Now unto thy bones good night!
Yearly will I do this rite.

PEDRO
Good morrow, masters. Put your torches out.
   The wolves have preyed, and look, the gentle day,
26 Before the wheels of Phoebus, round about
   Dapples the drowsy east with spots of gray.
Thanks to you all, and leave us. Fare you well.

CLAUDIO
Good morrow, masters. Each his several way.

PEDRO
30 Come, let us hence and put on other weeds,
   And then to Leonato's we will go.

CLAUDIO
32 And Hymen now with luckier issue speeds
   Than this for whom we rendered up this woe.

Exeunt.

*

∾ **V.4** *Enter Leonato, Benedick, [Beatrice,] Margaret,
Ursula, Old Man [Antonio], Friar [Francis], Hero.*

FRIAR
Did I not tell you she was innocent?

LEONATO
So are the prince and Claudio, who accused her

---

20 *utterèd* fully expressed   **26** *Phoebus* god who drives the chariot of the sun
30 *weeds* clothes (they are in mourning)   **32** *Hymen* god of marriage; *speeds*
(perhaps for "speed us")

Upon the error that you heard debated.   3
But Margaret was in some fault for this,
Although against her will, as it appears   5
In the true course of all the question.   6

ANTONIO
Well, I am glad that all things sorts so well.   7

BENEDICK
And so am I, being else by faith enforced   8
To call young Claudio to a reckoning for it.

LEONATO
Well, daughter, and you gentlewomen all,   10
Withdraw into a chamber by yourselves,
And when I send for you, come hither masked.
The prince and Claudio promised by this hour
To visit me. You know your office, brother:
You must be father to your brother's daughter,
And give her to young Claudio.   *Exeunt Ladies.*

ANTONIO
Which I will do with confirmed countenance.   17

BENEDICK
Friar, I must entreat your pains, I think.

FRIAR
To do what, signor?

BENEDICK
To bind me, or undo me – one of them.   20
Signor Leonato, truth it is, good signor,
Your niece regards me with an eye of favor.

LEONATO
That eye my daughter lent her. 'Tis most true.

BENEDICK
And I do with an eye of love requite her.

LEONATO
The sight whereof I think you had from me,
From Claudio, and the prince; but what's your will?

V.4 3 *Upon* because of   5 *against her will* unintentionally   6 *question* inves-
tigation   7 *sorts* turn out   8 *faith* fidelity to my word   17 *confirmed
countenance* straight face

BENEDICK
　　Your answer, sir, is enigmatical;
　　But, for my will, my will is your good will
　　May stand with ours, this day to be conjoined
30　In the state of honorable marriage,
　　In which, good friar, I shall desire your help.
LEONATO
　　My heart is with your liking.
FRIAR　　　　　　　　　　　　And my help.
　　Here comes the prince and Claudio.
　　　　Enter Prince [Don Pedro] and Claudio and two or
　　　　three other.
PEDRO
　　Good morrow to this fair assembly.
LEONATO
　　Good morrow, prince; good morrow, Claudio.
36　We here attend you. Are you yet determined
　　Today to marry with my brother's daughter?
CLAUDIO
38　I'll hold my mind, were she an Ethiope.
LEONATO
　　Call her forth, brother. Here's the friar ready.
　　　　　　　　　　　　　　　[Exit Antonio.]
PEDRO
40　Good morrow, Benedick. Why, what's the matter
　　That you have such a February face,
　　So full of frost, of storm, and cloudiness?
CLAUDIO
　　I think he thinks upon the savage bull.
　　Tush, fear not, man! We'll tip thy horns with gold,
45　And all Europa shall rejoice at thee,
46　As once Europa did at lusty Jove
　　When he would play the noble beast in love.

———

36 *yet* still　38 *Ethiope* i.e., black, and hence ugly in the stereotype comparison to blondes　45 *Europa* Europe　46 *Europa* a girl who was wooed by
Jove in the shape of a bull

BENEDICK
  Bull Jove, sir, had an amiable low,
  And some such strange bull leaped your father's cow
  And got a calf in that same noble feat   50
  Much like to you, for you have just his bleat.
     Enter [Leonato's] brother [Antonio], Hero, Beatrice,
     Margaret, Ursula [the ladies wearing masks].
CLAUDIO
  For this I owe you. Here comes other reck'nings.   52
  Which is the lady I must seize upon?
LEONATO
  This same is she, and I do give you her.   54
CLAUDIO
  Why then, she's mine. Sweet, let me see your face.
LEONATO
  No, that you shall not till you take her hand
  Before this friar and swear to marry her.
CLAUDIO
  Give me your hand before this holy friar.
  I am your husband if you like of me.
HERO   *[Unmasks.]*
  And when I lived I was your other wife;   60
  And when you loved you were my other husband.
CLAUDIO
  Another Hero!
HERO   Nothing certainer.
  One Hero died defiled; but I do live,   63
  And surely as I live, I am a maid.
PEDRO
  The former Hero! Hero that is dead!
LEONATO
  She died, my lord, but whiles her slander lived.

---

50 *calf* fool 52 *I owe you* I will pay you later (Benedick has managed to call
him both a calf and a bastard); *reck'nings* bills to pay 54 (editors often reject
Q and assign the speech to Antonio) 63 *defiled* disgraced (by the false
charge)

FRIAR

67   All this amazement can I qualify,
      When, after that the holy rites are ended,
69   I'll tell you largely of fair Hero's death.
70   Meantime let wonder seem familiar,
      And to the chapel let us presently.

BENEDICK
      Soft and fair, friar. Which is Beatrice?

BEATRICE   *[Unmasks.]*
      I answer to that name. What is your will?

BENEDICK
      Do not you love me?

BEATRICE   Why, no, no more than reason.

BENEDICK
      Why, then your uncle, and the prince, and Claudio
      Have been deceived – they swore you did.

BEATRICE
      Do not you love me?

BENEDICK   Troth, no, no more than reason.

BEATRICE
      Why, then my cousin, Margaret, and Ursula
      Are much deceived, for they did swear you did.

BENEDICK
80   They swore that you were almost sick for me.

BEATRICE
      They swore that you were well-nigh dead for me.

BENEDICK
      'Tis no such matter. Then you do not love me?

BEATRICE
83   No, truly, but in friendly recompense.

LEONATO
      Come, cousin, I am sure you love the gentleman.

CLAUDIO
      And I'll be sworn upon't that he loves her,

---

67 *qualify* moderate, relieve   69 *largely* in full   70 *let . . . familiar* treat this
marvel as if it were an ordinary matter   83 *friendly recompense* charitable re-
payment

For here's a paper written in his hand,
A halting sonnet of his own pure brain,
Fashioned to Beatrice.
HERO   And here's another,
Writ in my cousin's hand, stol'n from her pocket,
Containing her affection unto Benedick.   90
BENEDICK   A miracle! Here's our own hands against our   91
hearts. Come, I will have thee; but, by this light, I take
thee for pity.
BEATRICE   I would not deny you; but, by this good day, I
yield upon great persuasion, and partly to save your
life, for I was told you were in a consumption.
BENEDICK   Peace! I will stop your mouth.   97
    [Kisses her.]
PEDRO   How dost thou, Benedick, the married man?
BENEDICK   I'll tell thee what, prince: a college of wit-   99
crackers cannot flout me out of my humor. Dost thou   100
think I care for a satire or an epigram? No. If a man will
be beaten with brains, a shall wear nothing handsome   102
about him. In brief, since I do purpose to marry, I will
think nothing to any purpose that the world can say
against it; and therefore never flout at me for what I
have said against it, for man is a giddy thing, and this is   106
my conclusion. For thy part, Claudio, I did think to
have beaten thee; but in that thou art like to be my
kinsman, live unbruised, and love my cousin.
CLAUDIO   I had well hoped thou wouldst have denied   110
Beatrice, that I might have cudgeled thee out of thy
single life, to make thee a double-dealer, which out of   112
question thou wilt be if my cousin do not look exceeding narrowly to thee.

---

91 *hands* written testimony   **97** (Q assigns the line to Leonato, who may be
threatening to shut his niece up)   **99–100** *college of wit-crackers* assembly of
jokers   **102** *beaten with brains* defeated with witticisms (but with a play on
the literal sense of having brains flung at him, which will spoil his clothes)
106 *giddy* inconstant   **112** *double-dealer* married man, but also an unfaithful husband (a common newlywed joke)

BENEDICK   Come, come, we are friends. Let's have a
dance ere we are married, that we may lighten our own
hearts and our wives' heels.

LEONATO   We'll have dancing afterward.

119 BENEDICK   First, of my word! Therefore play, music.
120 Prince, thou art sad. Get thee a wife, get thee a wife!
121 There is no staff more reverend than one tipped with
horn.

Enter Messenger.

MESSENGER
My lord, your brother John is ta'en in flight,
And brought with armèd men back to Messina.

BENEDICK   Think not on him till tomorrow. I'll devise
thee brave punishments for him. Strike up, pipers!

Dance. [Exeunt.]

---

119 *of* upon   **121** *staff* rod of office, but also walking stick   **121–22** *tipped with horn* (the usual reference to horns and cuckoldry)

FOR THE BEST IN PAPERBACKS, LOOK FOR THE

The distinguished Pelican Shakespeare series, newly revised to be the premier choice for students, professors, and general readers well into the 21st century

All's Well That Ends Well
ISBN 0-14-071460-X

Antony and Cleopatra
ISBN 0-14-071452-9

As You Like It
ISBN 0-14-071471-5

The Comedy of Errors
ISBN 0-14-071474-X

Coriolanus
ISBN 0-14-071473-1

Cymbeline
ISBN 0-14-071472-3

Hamlet
ISBN 0-14-071454-5

Henry IV, Part I
ISBN 0-14-071456-1

Henry IV, Part 2
ISBN 0-14-071457-X

Henry V
ISBN 0-14-071458-8

Henry VI, Part 1
ISBN 0-14-071465-0

Henry VI, Part 2
ISBN 0-14-071466-9

Henry VI, Part 3
ISBN 0-14-071467-7

Henry VIII
ISBN 0-14-071475-8

Julius Caesar
ISBN 0-14-071468-5

King John
ISBN 0-14-071459-6

King Lear
ISBN 0-14-071476-6

King Lear (The Quarto and Folio Texts)
ISBN 0-14-071490-1

Love's Labor's Lost
ISBN 0-14-071477-4

Macbeth
ISBN 0-14-071478-2

Measure for Measure
ISBN 0-14-071479-0

The Merchant of Venice
ISBN 0-14-071462-6

The Merry Wives of Windsor
ISBN 0-14-071464-2

A Midsummer Night's Dream
ISBN 0-14-071455-3

Much Ado About Nothing
ISBN 0-14-071480-4

The Narrative Poems
ISBN 0-14-071481-2

Othello
ISBN 0-14-071463-4

Pericles
ISBN 0-14-071469-3

Richard II
ISBN 0-14-071482-0

Richard III
ISBN 0-14-071483-9

Romeo and Juliet
ISBN 0-14-071484-7

The Sonnets
ISBN 0-14-071453-7

The Taming of the Shrew
ISBN 0-14-071451-0

The Tempest
ISBN 0-14-071485-5

Timon of Athens
ISBN 0-14-071487-1

Titus Andronicus
ISBN 0-14-071491-X

Troilus and Cressida
ISBN 0-14-071486-3

Twelfth Night
ISBN 0-14-071489-8

The Two Gentlemen of Verona
ISBN 0-14-071461-8

The Winter's Tale
ISBN 0-14-071488-X

FOR THE BEST IN PAPERBACKS, LOOK FOR THE

In every corner of the world, on every subject under the sun, Penguin represents quality and variety—the very best in publishing today.

For complete information about books available from Penguin—including Puffins, Penguin Classics, and Compass—and how to order them, write to us at the appropriate address below. Please note that for copyright reasons the selection of books varies from country to country.

In the United Kingdom: Please write to *Dept. EP, Penguin Books Ltd, Bath Road, Harmondsworth, West Drayton, Middlesex UB7 0DA.*

In the United States: Please write to *Penguin Putnam Inc., P.O. Box 12289 Dept. B, Newark, New Jersey 07101-5289* or call 1-800-788-6262.

In Canada: Please write to *Penguin Books Canada Ltd, 10 Alcorn Avenue, Suite 300, Toronto, Ontario M4V 3B2.*

In Australia: Please write to *Penguin Books Australia Ltd, P.O. Box 257, Ringwood, Victoria 3134.*

In New Zealand: Please write to *Penguin Books (NZ) Ltd, Private Bag 102902, North Shore Mail Centre, Auckland 10.*

In India: Please write to *Penguin Books India Pvt Ltd, 11 Panchsheel Shopping Centre, Panchsheel Park, New Delhi 110 017.*

In the Netherlands: Please write to *Penguin Books Netherlands bv, Postbus 3507, NL-1001 AH Amsterdam.*

In Germany: Please write to *Penguin Books Deutschland GmbH, Metzlerstrasse 26, 60594 Frankfurt am Main.*

In Spain: Please write to *Penguin Books S. A., Bravo Murillo 19, 1° B, 28015 Madrid.*

In Italy: Please write to *Penguin Italia s.r.l., Via Benedetto Croce 2, 20094 Corsico, Milano.*

In France: Please write to *Penguin France, Le Carré Wilson, 62 rue Benjamin Baillaud, 31500 Toulouse.*

In Japan: Please write to *Penguin Books Japan Ltd, Kaneko Building, 2-3-25 Koraku, Bunkyo-Ku, Tokyo 112.*

In South Africa: Please write to *Penguin Books South Africa (Pty) Ltd, Private Bag X14, Parkview, 2122 Johannesburg.*